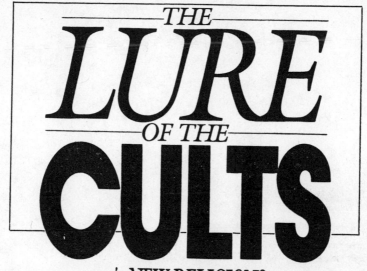

THE LURE OF THE CULTS

& NEW RELIGIONS

Why They Attract & What We Can Do

Ronald Enroth

INTERVARSITY PRESS
DOWNERS GROVE, ILLINOIS 60515

InterVarsity Press is the book-publishing division of InterVarsity Christian Fellowship, a student movement active on campus a hundreds of universities, colleges and schools of nursing. For information about local and regional activities, write Public Relations Dept., InterVarsity Christian Fellowship, 6400 Schroeder Rd., P.O. Box 7895, Madison, WI 53707-7895.

Distributed in Canada through InterVarsity Press, 860 Denison St., Unit 3, Markham, Ontario L3R 4H1, Canada.

All Scripture quotations, unless otherwise indicated, are from the Holy Bible, New International Version. Copyright © 1973, 1978, International Bible Society. Used by permission of Zondervan Bible Publishers.

Cover illustration: Roberta Polfus

ISBN 0-87784-994-3 (pbk.)
ISBN 0-8308-1708-5 (cloth)

Printed in the United States of America

Library of Congress Cataloging-in-Publication Data
Enroth, Ronald M.
   The lure of the cults & new religions.

   Includes bibliographies and index.
     1. Cults—Controversial literature.   2. Christian
sects—Controversial literature.   3. Evangelicalism.
I. Title.
BP603.E59 1987   291   87-17013
ISBN 0-8308-1708-6
ISBN 0-87784-994-3 (pbk.)

16	15	14	13	12	11	10	9	8	7	6	5	4	3	2	1
99	98	97	96	95	94	93	92	91	90	89	88	87			

To my mother

Acknowledgments

In preparing this book, I have benefited from a variety of sources. Without the assistance and interest of many parents, former cult members and fellow researchers in the field of new religious movements, this project would not have been successful. I am especially indebted to the Spiritual Counterfeits Project staff and to my colleague at Westmont College, Ned Divelbiss.

Special thanks to Jim Sire of IVP for his incredible patience.

My wife and daughters were supportive, as usual, despite the constant telephone calls and other interruptions in our lives as a result of my research in this very current topic.

ONE

After Jonestown

I n November 1978 the nation and the world were jolted during an unforgettable few days by news reports which described the horrible events occurring in the remote jungle of Guyana, South America. Jim Jones had always wanted to be remembered in history, and that wish was being fulfilled in one of the most gruesome tragedies of modern times. The innocuous jungle encampment— appropriately named Jonestown—soon became etched in the minds of millions as a place where more than nine hundred men, women and children had experienced the ultimate form of cultic victimization. Following the directions of Jones, they drank Kool-Aid laced with cyanide and died.

Since Jonestown the word *cult* has assumed new significance on the American scene. In countless articles, interviews and editorial pages, the public has been made aware of the reality and destructive potential of religious-political groups that manipulate the mind, subvert the will and vandalize the soul. The unprecedented media exposure given Jonestown has alerted Americans to the fact that seemingly beneficent religious groups can mask a hellish rot. Most people find it difficult to believe that not all religion is benign. The People's Temple tragedy reminds us that religious evil is the worst form of evil, for it masquerades in a social form that we have come to associate with all that is good and decent and ennobling.

The New Religious Entrepreneurs

There have always been charlatans who have lined their own pockets in the name of religion. The American religious landscape has never been without its Elmer Gantrys and Marjoe Gortners. These hallelujah hucksters have at least been blatantly obvious about their real objectives. The new religious entrepreneurs, on the other hand, often beguile the public and unsuspecting recruits with their promises of psychic self-improvement, "blissed out" salvation, unbounded awareness and abundant living. On first glance, they appear to be so legitimate, so convincing, so relevant, so humanitarian.

The cults of the eighties are, like Jim Jones's organization, masters of public relations. They market their spiritual wares with all the expertise and planning of Madison Avenue executives. They covet, strive for and sometimes achieve respectability and public acceptance. While some of the smaller separatist groups shun approval by the prevailing religious establishment, none of the new religious movements wants the label "cult." None desires the shame of a Jonestown. Because of adverse media publicity, many are seeking to change their images, adjust their masks.

Yet on close scrutiny, we see that the mask is still there. The attempt to package, conceal, mollify and modify their message must be viewed as just another dimension of the deception that is at the heart of all false religion. The deceit of the promoters is not always conscious; it is often the result of sincere desire to do good and intense commitment to a cause. For the rank-and-file cult member, it may be a strategy adopted after prolonged exposure to a religious system in which the end justifies the means.

From the perspective of biblical Christianity, the new cultic movements that have emerged during the past twenty years or so must be viewed as spiritual counterfeits. They represent "other gospels" that the New Testament repeatedly warns against. All counterfeits are copies of that which is good, valued and effective. God's adversary, Satan, does not claim to be evil. He is not up-front about his real intentions. Ever since his first exploits in Eden, he has been the archdeceiver. He often lurks behind a benign persona, dressed in alluring religious garb.

Writing in *The New York Times Book Review*, Dr. James S. Gordon concluded: "The final horror of Jonestown is that one man counterfeiting Christianity and social democracy could attract, hold, and annihilate so many who wanted and needed so much and meant so well."[1] All of us wonder how such a thing could happen. Why do people so easily follow a demagogue? What is the appeal of high-intensity religious groups?

Exploring the Appeal
Large numbers of Americans, particularly young adults, have been attracted to unconventional religious movements and quasi-religious self-discovery cults. It is the aim of this book to analyze the lure of cultic groups and to explain the significance of such phenomena for the individual, the family, the church and society. This book is not intended to be an exhaustive treatment of the topic, nor does it claim complete neutrality. It is written as much to warn as to inform.

I write from the perspective of an evangelical Christian. I believe that God has revealed himself in the person of his Son, Jesus Christ, and that his Word, the Bible, serves as the ultimate authority for determining truth and error. This means that I have firm personal convictions about the beliefs and practices of the various groups discussed in this book. At the same time, it is my hope that the book will be informed by scholarship and reflect the insights of behavioral scientists and other professionals who are familiar with new religious movements.

Long before Jonestown I had researched and written about extremist and unconventional religious groups. Much of the information that has been reported about the People's Temple has corroborated the findings and conclusions about cultic groups published earlier. Many of the groups referred to in the pages that follow are well known to those already familiar with the literature in print on new religious movements. A few of the groups discussed here will be new to most readers. Some are small organizations. It should be remembered that prior to November 1978 the People's Temple was also a small, relatively unknown band of "true believers."

Our purpose is to examine common characteristics of the new religious sects and to determine the principles by which they and their leaders operate. We shall attempt to discover why such groups appeal to so many young adults and why we dare not dismiss them as mere fads. The nature of the book is such that a detailed analysis of individual groups is not possible. Generalizations will be made, which tend to be negatively described by critics as "sweeping." A word of explanation is therefore in order.

As a sociologist I am interested in looking for patterned behavior in social phenomena. Recurrent patterns help us bring order to a vast amount of data. Those of us who have studied the new religious movements have observed remarkable clusters of traits that seem to cut across so many of the groups, despite their obvious individual distinctions. Although there are always dangers in lumping together the characteristics of groups of any kind, it is instructive and useful to devise concepts and to look for commonalities in order to get a handle on what otherwise might be a confused and cluttered scene.

To protect the privacy of individuals whose personal experiences are related at various points throughout the book, I have not used their actual names.

TWO

The Many Faces of Cultism

A policeman in Arlington, Washington, noticed a burned-out taillight on an old sedan and signaled the driver to pull off the road. While performing a routine check, he asked to see a driver's license. The driver indicated that he did not have one. The officer discovered that the man and his passenger did not have any traditional form of identification. He learned that they were members of a religious cult known as the Church of Armageddon (also known as the Love Family) that requires adherents to discard their original names and assume biblical names of virtue like Strength, Diligence and Noble. The driver refused to give his former name and date of birth. He and his friend explained that they were eternal beings and had no birth dates.

In Billings, Montana, an infant girl was born dead in a bathtub when an extremist religious group known as the Overcomers re-fused to obtain medical help for the mother after complications developed. Two male members of the group later took the baby to a hospital emergency room, where nurses were told that the child was stillborn. Authorities were notified, and an investigation for criminal negligence was launched. Members of the group refuse any form of medical care, including eyeglasses.

Joan Padillo (not her real name) was a student at the University of California—Berkeley. One night she stepped outside the study center in her dorm and lit a cigarette. She struck up a conversation with two young men who were sitting nearby. "We got into heavy philosophical stuff about God and the purpose of life. They kind of interested me because nobody had ever asked me my opinion about those kinds of things."

The young men said they were associated with an organization known as the Creative Community Project, and they invited her to a free dinner at the communal house in which they lived. Joan was a vulnerable person for a number of reasons. "I was really unhappy and feeling basically alone. My roommate and I didn't get along so well. I had a lot of trouble making friends because people at that school are really academic. All they wanted to do was read books. I was beginning to falter in school, and I panicked."

Joan accepted the dinner invitation and eventually ended up at an indoctrination camp of the Unification Church. "It was like I was looking for love and I found it." She dropped out of the university, was assigned to a mobile fund-raising team, and started selling candy and flowers on the streets with other Moonies. She brought in between $90 to $160 a day on the average. "When I was fund-raising, I would see people doing just ordinary things like driving a car, listening to the radio, talking to each other. I would think, 'Gee, it's been six months since I've done that.' I would get to look inside houses and see kids, cats, dogs—the whole thing. And I would think to myself, 'I'm never going to have that kind of life.'"

Laura Morrow was a college sophomore when she became interested in the Divine Light Mission, an Eastern mystical cult headed by Guru Maharaj Ji. She states that she had taken drugs in high school and college. While at college, she practiced yoga and transcendental meditation. "I decided to quit drugs completely, but I was still searching for something. I was attracted to the experience that the DLM offered. His representatives said there was a meditation I could do all the time that would put me in contact with my true self and give me peace of mind."

Laura joined the movement, sought after and received what is termed in the group "the Knowledge," and became a "premic," a follower of a god in the flesh—Guru Maharaj Ji. Each morning and evening before meditation, Laura would sing a devotional song to him—the Perfect Master. A picture of Maharaj Ji would be on the altar, and a cup of water that had been placed on the altar would be passed around. The cup contained holy water that had been touched by the Guru's feet. "That would be passed around and we would drink from it."

What Is a Cult?

These four brief accounts of cultic involvement illustrate the diversity of the new religious movements in America. There is no way of accurately determining how many cults presently are functioning in the United States and Canada. Estimates range from many hundreds to thousands. There are probably dozens of groups with fewer than fifty members. On the other hand, there are probably only a few organizations with memberships over fifty thousand. Just how many cults exist depends in large part on how far the definitional net is cast. The Transcendental Meditation movement, for example, asserts that TM is a nonreligious meditation technique with educational and therapeutic value. On October 17, 1977, a federal court in New Jersey declared that the TM movement of Maharishi Mahesh Yogi *is* religious in nature. Since Transcendental Meditation is perhaps the largest and fastest-growing of the Eastern spiritual disciplines that have emerged in the United States in recent years, the head count of cultists swelled considerably as a result of that judicial precedent.

As psychologist Margaret Singer points out, the word *cult* is necessarily subject to individual judgment. "It has been variously applied to groups involved in beliefs and practices just off the beat of traditional religions; to groups making exploratory excursions into non-Western philosophical practices; and to groups involving intense relationships between followers and a powerful idea or leader."[1]

Scholars disagree on the precise definition of what Professor Roy Wallis calls "this elusive and slippery concept."[2] Most sociologists of religion note that cults represent a break with the mainstream of the religious tradition of the society in which they exist. Professors Rodney Stark and William Bainbridge identify two types of deviant religious groups: sects and cults. Sects are schismatic groups—that is, they have a prior link with another religious body. Sects present themselves as the revitalized, authentic, restored version of the faith from which they split. Cults, on the other hand, do not have a prior organizational tie with a "parent" religious body. A cult may represent an alien or imported religion, or it may be a domestic, though totally new, form of religious expression.[3]

The origin of the word may be traced to the Latin *cultus,* which connotes all that is involved in worship—ritual, emotion, liturgy, attitude. A "pop" variation of this basic meaning can be seen in such expressions as "football cult," "Elvis Presley cult," or "Hitler cult." Religious cult members often regard their leaders as gods, avatars or messianic figures. In this sense the designation "Moon cult" is indeed descriptive and accurate.

For the Christian, the concept of cult must also include another crucial dimension—the theological. It is my view that any group, movement or teaching may be considered cultic to the degree that it deviates from biblical, orthodox Christianity. God's objective truth, as revealed in Scripture, is the standard for evaluating all belief and practice. Viewing a cult as "a deviation from orthodoxy" may be of dubious value to the secular observer of cults, but this frame of reference is vital to the Christian who is concerned about discerning truth from error. The conviction that one has a firm framework of truth by which to evaluate the claims of other groups is seen as presumptuous and constricting by the non-Christian. But the Bible reminds us to "test the spirits to see whether they are from God" (1 Jn 4:1).

Brooks Alexander, co-founder of the Spiritual Counterfeits Project, employs the theological perspective in his discussion of the two core characteristics of all cultic teachings:

1. *A false or inadequate basis of salvation.* The apostle Paul drew a distinction that is utterly basic to our understanding of truth when he said, "By grace are you saved through faith; and that not of yourselves; it is the gift of God: not of works lest any man should boast" (Eph 2:8-9). Inasmuch as *the* central doctrine of biblical Christianity is the sacrificial death of Christ for our sin, all cultic deviations tend to downplay the finished work of Christ and emphasize the importance of earning moral acceptance before God through our own righteous works *as a basis of salvation.*

2. *A false basis of authority.* Biblical Christianity by definition takes the Bible as its yardstick of the true, the false, the necessary, the permitted, the forbidden, and the irrelevant. Cults, on the other hand, commonly resort to extra-biblical documents or contemporary "revelation" as the substantial basis of their theology (e.g., Mormons). While some cult groups go through the motions of accepting the authority of Scripture, they actually honor the group's or leader's novel *interpretation* of Scripture as normative (e.g.: Jehovah's Witnesses, The Way International).[4]

To sort out and distinguish between the many faces of cultism, the following scheme is offered as one method of classification which, while useful, is admittedly incomplete. Five basic categories of new religious movements are presented: (1) Eastern mystical groups,

(2) aberrant Christian groups, (3) psychospiritual or self-improvement groups, (4) eclectic-syncretistic groups, and (5) psychic-occult-astral groups.

The general characteristics of each category will be identified and representative groups from each category sketched briefly. The reader should be cautioned that this listing will be far from complete. It is not an inclusive catalog of cultic movements. Also, a number of the new religious groups could easily be placed in more than one category. To avoid possible confusion created by overlap, each group will be located in the classification scheme according to its focal themes and dominant thrust.

Eastern Mystical Groups

North America is currently fascinated with Eastern philosophy and religion. It is estimated that more than two million Americans are actively involved in some Eastern cult or spiritual discipline. This Eastern invasion is typified by groups which stress a subjective approach to truth and which value experience over reason and doctrine. These new mysticisms teach the essential oneness of the universe—that God, man and nature share the same divine essence. Their objective is to help the individual become aware of the divine nature within. "Look within; thou *art* Buddha" is a guiding principle of Zen Buddhism, for example.

The Hare Krishna Movement. Perhaps the best known of the Eastern cults because of their bright saffron robes and shaved heads, these chanting devotees are part of a movement that has experienced steady and sometimes dramatic growth in many parts of the world. With a view toward establishing and disseminating in the Western world a lifestyle based on the Vedic scriptures, this Hindu sect was formed in 1966 in New York City by an Indian swami, A. C. Bhaktivedanta. Stressing devotion to the god Krishna, devotees reject the material indulgences of the West and despise establishment religions, which they view as hypocritical and compromising. The sect's official name is the International Society for Krishna

Consciousness (ISKCON). Their founder died in 1977 and the work of the movement is being carried forward by the cooperative efforts of a group of his advanced disciples.

Zen Buddhism. Zen represents a tradition of spiritual and psychological disciplines originating in the Orient and popularized in America by Alan Watts. The goal of Zen is the achieving of a state of peace and enlightenment known as *satori*. Zen shuns doctrine in favor of intuition and a direct experience of the Absolute. It is existential and anti-intellectual, appealing to youthful seekers who are turned off by what they perceive as the rationalized and restricted religions of the West.

The Divine Light Mission. This meditation-oriented cult reached its zenith in the United States in 1973 when thousands of followers of Guru Maharaj Ji, then fifteen years old, gathered in Houston's Astrodome to hear the plump "Perfect Master" promise to end human suffering and bring a thousand years of peace. Headquartered in Miami, the Mission's membership is reportedly on the decline. Followers, known as "premies," learn how to receive "the Knowledge" from the Guru or one of his lieutenants (mahatmas). Many live in ashrams, although the trend seems to be away from communal living and toward conventional family living in the larger society. Today the Guru lives quietly with his wife and two children in relative obscurity in a hilltop mansion overlooking the Pacific in Malibu, California.

Healthy-Happy-Holy Organization (3HO). Coming from a tradition of kundalini yoga, this cultic group of several thousand committed members is based on the Sikh religion, a combination of Hinduism and Islam. As one observer noted, 3HO was "created on American soil out of American and Indian elements" in 1969 by a yoga master known as Yogi Bhajan. The organization stresses communal living, vegetarian diet and the achievement of spiritual enlightenment through various techniques, chanting and meditation.

Soka Gakkai—also known as Nichiren Shoshu (NSA). Imported

from Japan, this Buddhist derivative sect is growing rapidly in several countries and is known for its extremism and intolerance. In contrast to other Eastern groups which advocate self-denial, NSA stresses ambition and the acquisition of wealth and power in the here and now. Headquartered in Santa Monica, California, the organization manufactures home altars and shrines and operates extensive printing plants. It publishes weekly and monthly magazines, pamphlets and newspapers in both Japanese and English. Large meetings of chanting followers often conclude with a flourish of music and marching led by vigorous fanwavers.

Ananda Marga. There are an estimated seventy-five thousand Ananda Marga (meaning "the path of bliss") devotees in the United States, who employ meditation techniques and yoga with the ultimate goal of achieving self-realization or "cosmic consciousness." The group combines its religious philosophy and practices with various social service and humanitarian activities like free food distribution, disaster relief and literacy training. Critics of Ananda Marga allege the movement is fascist.

Meher Baba Movement. This small (about seven thousand members) Eastern cult was founded by a now-deceased Indian leader who claimed to be an avatar or savior. His basic teaching emphasizes a common theme running through many of the New Age religions—that reality consists of a single, undifferentiated unity. "We are all one." Followers, or "Baba Lovers," also believe in reincarnation, Karma and the illusory nature of all sensate experience.

Self-Realization Fellowship (SRF). This Hindu sect was brought to the United States in 1920 by Paramahansa Yogananda. Headquartered in Los Angeles, California, SRF's ultimate objective is to unite the individual with God in a state of pure bliss through yoga meditative techniques.

Aberrant Christian Groups

In a very general sense, the religious groups within this classification identify with the dominant religious tradition of North America and therefore, according to sociological criteria, are not cultic movements. Although all claim to be biblically based and Christian, many deviate—in terms of social practice or doctrine or both—from what is conventionally understood to be conservative Protestant evangelicalism. They are sectlike fringe movements which are closer to the margins of mainstream Christian denominations than other religious groups discussed in this book.

Included in this category are organizations like the River of Life Ministry (founded by Ed Mitchell), the Body of Christ (founded by Marie Kolasinski), the Mizpah Brethren and Community Chapel (Seattle), as well as dozens of smaller groups little known outside their immediate locale.

A major thesis of this book is that cultlike manifestations are not restricted to exotic Eastern religions or widely publicized groups like the Unification Church of Sun Myung Moon. Deviations from Christian orthodoxy as well as unconventional practices can be found right around the corner from the First Presbyterian Church or the First Baptist Church in groups that use the label "Christian."

The Family of Love—formerly the Children of God. Under the leadership of Moses David, or "Mo" (real name: David Berg), this communal group, claiming to be made up of born-again Christians, has become a worldwide movement of members. Berg is a self-styled end-time prophet who communicates to his flock largely by means of his controversial "Mo Letters." The group espouses strong anti-establishment views and highly unconventional notions concerning sex. Female members are encouraged to witness for Christ by engaging in "flirty fishing," a form of religious prostitution. The organization is not currently active in North America but maintains a vigorous outreach in South America, Asia and parts of Europe.

Alamo Christian Church. Known in its early days as the Tony and Susan Alamo Christian Foundation, this organization originated in Southern California in the heyday of the Jesus movement. In recent years the scene of the action has shifted to Alma, Arkansas, where the organization operates several businesses in addition to its soul-saving activities. After Susan's death from cancer, devoted followers prayed beside her coffin in pairs twenty-four hours a day for months, expecting God to resurrect her. Tony has since remarried. The organization's missionaries have distributed strongly anti-Catholic leaflets in major cities throughout the United States. It has also been embroiled in legal battles with the U.S. Department of Labor and with parents of some members.

The Church of Bible Understanding. Headed by a fifty-one-year-old authoritarian prophet and leader, Stewart Traill, this group consists of several communal "fellowships" throughout the northeastern United States and Canada. As is true of so many groups, accurate membership figures are hard to come by, but estimates go as high as three thousand and as low as five hundred. The organization runs a janitorial business, reportedly employing several hundred church members at low wages. Traill, a former vacuum cleaner salesman, has experienced increased criticism from disaffected members because of his affluent lifestyle.

The Love Family—the Church of Armageddon. The founder and recently deposed leader of several hundred members of the Love Family is Love Israel, formerly known as Paul Erdman. The group owns properties in the Seattle area and has established a small colony in Hawaii. It shuns outside medical care and became controversial several years ago when at least two members died after inhaling toluene, an industrial solvent, as part of a religious ritual. The group's charter states, "The Kingdom of God is a state of love, a family that can never end, the Love Family. Our family surname is Israel. Our duty is to show mankind that Love Is Real." Observers believe that the organization is now in decline.

Faith Assembly. Founded by former seminary professor Dr. Hobart Freeman, this extremist Christian group teaches the necessity of having "total faith in God in all things." Such faith will make unnecessary the use of "secondary supports" like doctors, medication and all forms of insurance. According to Freeman's teaching,

Christians bring shame to the body of Christ by consulting physicians and submitting to surgeons' hands. The group believes that using prescribed drugs for medical purposes opens the door to control by demonic powers. Authorities report that as many as ninety deaths (many of them children) in eleven states since 1975 have been linked to Freeman's teachings. The controversial pastor died in 1984 of severe cardiovascular disease and mild bronchopneumonia at the age of sixty-four. Faith Assembly is not associated with the Assemblies of God denomination.

The Church of the Living Word—"The Walk." At least one hundred churches around the United States are affiliated with this "restoration movement" founded by "Apostle" John Robert Stevens. Members receive guidance from and submit to the elders and the "apostolic company" who regularly receive "new levels of revelation" from the Lord. Much emphasis is given to binding Satan, spiritual warfare and the significance of physical "body signs." Critics charge that some church practices involve psychic phenomena and border on the occult. Since Stevens's death, some members claim to have communicated with him in the spirit world.

The Way International. Called a Bible research and teaching organization by its zealous supporters, the Way revolves around the teaching of one man, Victor Paul Wierwille, who was affectionately known as "the Doctor" by Wayers. Claiming to have the only correct interpretation of the Word since the first century, Wierwille dispensed his heretical teachings through a series of videotaped courses, the first of which is a widely advertised "Power for Abundant Living" course (required donation: one hundred dollars). The title of one of Wierwille's books, *Jesus Christ Is Not God,* is a clue to the group's basic theological orientation. The organization is critical of traditional churches and meets in private homes rather than in conventional church buildings. They have been especially active near military bases and have attracted high-school students through various musical groups.

The Christ Family. Headed by a man known as "Lightning

Amen," this nomadic group believes it is the only true body of Christ's followers in the world today. Members all take the last name Christ (for example, Martha Christ, Bill Christ) and live in temporary encampments, mainly in the western half of the United States. They dress in long white robes and carry bedrolls over their shoulders as they trek across America. They believe their leader to be a reincarnation of Christ. Their primary message consists of three taboos: no sex, no materialism and no killing (they are vegetarians and do not wear leather products). Marijuana use is acceptable (they call it "God's tranquilizer") since God created the marijuana plant.

Psychospiritual or Self-Improvement Groups
A host of new mind/body therapies have blended into the stream of America's consumerism in recent years. Some, like MSIA (Movement of Spiritual Inner Awareness), PSI World and Scientology, have focused on psychospiritual concerns; others, like biofeedback, meditation and acupuncture, are primarily directed at improving overall health and psychic well-being. Interest in mind/body interaction is illustrated by the growing popularity of bioenergetics, rolfing, reflexology, therapeutic touch and other practices associated with the holistic health movement.

The decade of the sixties was the period when large numbers of Americans embarked on a journey of self-discovery and self-improvement through what came to be known as the Human Potential Movement. Inevitably, as Conway and Siegelman point out, "This rich new world of personal growth became subject to exploitation and abuse. . . . America's searchers, in their earnest longing to find something higher and their sincere desire for self-improvement, had no way of interpreting their experiences, of separating the truly spiritual from the sham, or of distinguishing genuine personal growth from artificially induced sensation."[5]

The 1970s and 80s have seen even more interest in self-actualization and personal transformation. There has been a proliferation of what sociologists Stark and Bainbridge call "client cults," in which people pursue self-improvement and unlimited human potential—for a price. From the Christian perspective, such activity must be viewed in light of human fallenness and our innate inability to please a holy God. Because of sin and self, it is more appropriate to speak of humankind's lack of potential apart from the mercy and grace of God in Jesus Christ.

Synanon. Started as a "therapeutic community" for drug rehabilitation over two decades ago by Charles (Chuck) Dederich, this one-time "model" organization has developed into a new religious movement in recent years. Controversy has swirled about the California based alternative lifestyle organization amid charges of authoritarianism, child abuse and violence.

Arica Training. Arica is a system of spiritual techniques drawn from various Eastern disciplines, developed by Oscar Ichazo and named for his hometown, Arica, Chile. Practiced intensely, Arica exercises promise "the complete realization of a human being."

The Forum—formerly est. During a thirteen-year period beginning in 1971, nearly 500,000 people enrolled in Werner Erhard's sixty-hour training seminars called "est" (Erhard Seminars Training). In January 1985, est underwent cosmetic changes and emerged as the Forum, designed for people who "got it together" in the seventies and who are interested in "making it happen" in the eighties. The self-awareness program costs $525 for two consecutive weekends and one evening follow-up session. Like its predecessor, the Forum's basic focus is derived from Eastern thought and is heavily experiential in nature. It is advertised as "a powerful, practical inquiry into the issues that determine our personal effectiveness." It promises to put people in touch with "being" and "aliveness."

Transcendental Meditation (TM). Maharishi Mahesh Yogi, the founder of TM, and his growing number of followers claim that Transcendental Meditation is the ultimate solution to all problems facing humanity and the world today. They deny that TM is a religion or a philosophy and emphasize that it is a "natural, easy, systematic, and scientifically verified technique." From the perspective of the Christian, Harris Langford's concise definition says it all:

Transcendental Meditation is a diluted strain of Hinduism with some very specific Hindu worship features, but couched in terms which actually hide its religious basis from most of the Maharishi's disciples. It is westernized Hinduism, expressed in scientific terms but with the strict discipline removed, and offered to Americans who are empty of spirit.[6]

Lifespring. Founded in 1974 by John Hanley, Lifespring resembles other human potential or "growth" organizations with an emphasis on subjective experience and the individual's absolute sovereignty over the universe. Lifespring asserts that individuals experience problems because of false beliefs about themselves and reality. By taking Lifespring courses, one breaks down obstructing previous belief systems and then begins to build a new life and a new image of reality.

Scientology. The Church of Scientology promises magical powers and the increase of individual ability through a combination of lay psychotherapy, Eastern philosophy and the personal views of the organization's founder, L. Ron Hubbard. Scientology bills itself as an applied religious philosophy offering the would-be follower "total knowledge" and "total freedom." The writings of the movement are filled with highly specialized, scientific-sounding jargon. In recent years the organization has received much publicity because of its legal problems with various governmental agencies such as the FBI and the IRS. Scientologists claim they are being persecuted and denied freedom of religion. Hubbard, author of the book *Dianetics: The Modern Science of Mental Health,* spent his last years as a mysterious recluse worth millions and died in 1986 at the age of seventy-four.

Eclectic-Syncretistic Groups
Some of the new religious movements attempt to distill elements

or truths from several different spiritual or mystical traditions and reformulate those differing elements into a single religious system. By putting together new formulations of "truth" (syncretism), selected from various sources (eclecticism), they can achieve, from their perspective, the best of all spiritual worlds.

The Unification Church. Perhaps the best-known group in this category is the Unification Church of Sun Myung Moon. Its ultimate aim is the unification not only of world Christianity but also of virtually *all* religions—East and West. The theology and religious practices of the "Moonies" reflect elements of Oriental philosophy and mysticism as well as traditional Christianity—some of them distortions, to be sure. Mr. Moon's followers have been criticized for their recruitment, indoctrination and fundraising methods as well as their involvement in political and economic affairs. Membership estimates range from five thousand to fifteen thousand in the United States, and hundreds of thousands in Asia, especially in Korea, the founder's homeland. Devout disciples believe that Moon is the "Lord of the Second Advent," the messiah figure promised in the group's revelatory scripture, *Divine Principle.*

The Church Universal and Triumphant. This organization, headed by Elizabeth Clare Prophet ("Guru Ma" to her followers), proclaims "the coming revolution in higher consciousness" with the help of "ascended masters." The church believes in reincarnation and Ms. Prophet claims that the late Pope John XXIII dictated a message to her from the spirit world conveying the authority for the Church Universal and Triumphant. Spiritual significance is attributed to sound and color, and members engage in high-speed chants called decrees. The group's teaching has been described by Mark Albrecht as an "all-embracing monistic-mystical system of eclectic occultism" resulting in a "systematic inversion of biblical truth through Gnostic reinterpretation of Scripture and carefully orchestrated syncretism."[7] Because of its heavy involvement in occult and spiritist practices, this cult could be cross-classified under

31

our fifth category, Psychic-Occult-Astral Groups.

Eckankar (ECK). Eckankar advertises itself as a "direct path to God" that encompasses all of man's religions. The ECK teachings supposedly provide a "way of life" based on "the most ancient religion known to man" as expressed by the spiritual guidance of the "Living ECK Master." The route to self-realization and God-realization is said to be via "the ancient science of soul travel." From the Christian perspective, this amounts to nothing less than "a restatement of classical gnosticism, eclectically trimmed with concepts and symbols from various occult systems."[8]

Baha'i. Baha'i is a Persian cult that began among the Sufis in the mid-nineteenth century. Its belief system combines the teachings of all major Eastern religions and emphasizes the concepts of love and unity. Baha'i is not new to the American religious scene, having been introduced at a world parliament of religions held in Chicago in 1893. Recently it has experienced a resurgence of interest and growth, due in part to publicity given it by several popular entertainers. There are currently about one thousand Baha'i assemblies in the United States, most of them concentrated in large population centers.

Sufism. The origins of the Sufi sect are in mystical Islam and Hinduism. Sufis are said to be "at home in all religions." This highly syncretistic sect teaches that there is a secret teaching within all religions. It stresses meditative techniques and bodily movement as avenues of opening up the mind to cosmic dimensions, to "the attainment of the infinite spirit."

Psychic-Occult-Astral Groups
The growth of cults in recent years has been accompanied by a new preoccupation with psychic and occult phenomena and a revival of interest in various forms of astral religion. The prevailing cultural ethos of alienation and spiritual impotence has provoked a flight to worlds beyond the ordinary realm of knowing, to the occult or "hidden" teachings of "ancient masters." Perhaps in reaction

against our overly scientific or technological society, men and women are increasingly looking to the stars and consulting astrological charts for personal guidance and spiritual direction.

The Aetherius Society. The British founder of the Aetherius Society, Dr. George King, has a long history of involvement in psychic activity, Eastern mysticism and traditional spiritualism. He was deeply immersed in kundalini and other forms of yoga when he received word in 1954 that he had been chosen by the "Cosmic Intelligences" to be their "Primary Terrestrial Channel" for significant messages they were about to transmit to earth. This was the beginning of a whole series of transmissions from the Space Masters which have been recorded and circulated by King and his society. King claims to have contacted "Master Jesus," who commissioned him to "act as an essential link between Earth and the Higher Forces." After a successful lecture tour in the United States speaking to various flying-saucer, metaphysical and theosophical groups, King took up residence in California.

UFO Cults. Several smaller groups, claiming regular contact with space beings aboard flying saucers, have emerged during the flurry of reported UFO sightings in recent years. One such group, which received considerable media coverage, was headed by a mysterious couple calling themselves Bo and Peep, or simply, "the Two." Like other UFO groups, this one proclaimed a message of coming gloom and catastrophe for earth people. In order to escape and to achieve eternal life, members were asked to abandon friends and family, sell all material possessions and prepare for the great astral trip.

Association for Research and Enlightenment. This organization was founded by the well-known psychic Edgar Cayce in Virginia Beach, Virginia, in 1931. While in a trance, Cayce claimed to be able to describe a person's previous lives. Famous for his views on reincarnation, Cayce also predicted the future and diagnosed diseases while in a trance state.

Astrology. Not so much a cult which one joins but a loosely organized network of practitioners providing occult services, astrology is popular with Americans. In a 1976 Gallup poll, twenty-two per cent of a national sample answered yes when asked, "Do you believe in astrology, or not?" Of the college-educated persons polled, eighty-five per cent claimed to know the sign under which they had been born.[9] Astrology derives from ancient astral religions that taught that the planets and stars influence human activity.

Some of the groups mentioned in this five-part classification are new only in the sense that they have emerged from relative inactivity and obscurity to blossom in the conducive cultural climate of recent decades. Others, like the Hare Krishna movement, are new imports to the West but represent a well-established religious tradition in another society. Finally, any comprehensive examination of cult phenomena would require the addition of one more category to those already listed: Established Cults. Included under this heading would be groups like the Mormon Church, Christian Science and Jehovah's Witnesses. All three of these were new religious movements of nineteenth-century America. Because the focus of this book is on the newer cultic movements and because abundant literature—both Christian and secular—already exists with regard to these established cults, they will not be discussed here.

The more general labels used to describe the previously described groups have included New-Age religion, sect, new religious movement, and the more popularly used term for bizarre or unusual groups, cult. The word *cult* means many things to many people. True, it has assumed a pejorative connotation in recent years, largely as a result of media usage. But it remains a neutral term in the scholarly literature of the behavioral sciences—sociology, psychology and anthropology.

The semantic handle applied to a given religious group is not as significant as our understanding of its social organization, beliefs and practices. Since this book is directed to a wide readership and assumes little prior knowledge of the topic on the part of at least some readers, I shall freely use a variety of designations when referring to new religious movements. When the word *cult* is used, I do not intend to convey disrespect or derogation. A negative evaluation of any given group does not mean a lack of commitment on the part of the author to religious freedom and the right of any group to freely promote its beliefs. The United States has a rich history of religious diversity and, as a citizen and as a Christian believer, I am committed to the preservation of pluralism. The same First Amendment which provides freedom of religion for all, however, also protects the right of free speech, including the right to critique and disagree with the religious beliefs and practices of others. Negative evaluation is not a synonym for "attack" and opposing opinion should not be reinterpreted as "anti-religious" or cited as evidence of intolerance—a strategy that, unfortunately, has sometimes been used by some groups mentioned in this book.

THREE

The Dawn
of the
New Age

W e are the heralds of a New Age. Scientology . . . is a passport to this new time." Those are the words of L. Ron Hubbard, founder of the Church of Scientology, one of the most widely discussed and most controversial of the new religious movements. It is essentially the same theme promulgated by many of the new religious groups—that humankind is on the threshold of, or has already entered into, a new era in human history, a new spiritual age which will require new modes of thinking, new revelation, new truth. For this reason many cultic movements describe themselves as New Age religions.

The Age of Aquarius
In a world which they view as undergoing fundamental change,

these groups stress the need to be attuned to the "new religious consciousness," to join and flow with the forces of change and to lead the way in discovering new forms of religious experience. One such group is the Healthy-Happy-Holy Organization (3HO), which teaches that we are now witnessing the end of the "Piscean Age" and entering the "Aquarian Age."

One observer describes the cultural shifts which 3HO foresees: "The change will be from material to spiritual concerns, from factionalism to a pervasive sense of human unity, from the present dominance of 'individual consciousness' to a 'group consciousness' and 'God consciousness'; in short, we shall see the beginning of a truly spiritual global culture."[1]

The Dawn of the Messianic Age is the title of a flyer advertising a special seminar on the teachings of Sun Myung Moon of the Unification Church. The Moonies teach that we are living in a new age which began in 1960. According to Unification theology, human history can be divided into three ages: the Old Testament Age, the New Testament Age and the Completed Testament Age. They believe that God dispenses truth according to the spiritual and intellectual levels of people at any given time in history. The Bible was adequate for those people in the past for whom it was meant. In this highly sophisticated technological age, however, an even higher level of truth is required than is found in the New Testament. Thus, according to the Moonies, this "new truth" for the "new age" can be found in the *Divine Principle*, the book which contains the special revelation given to Mr. Moon.

The *Divine Principle* suggests that modern men and women who are capable of perceiving spiritual things will respond to New Age truth "even though they may face discrepancies between the new view of truth and that of the old age."[2] In today's world, according to Moon's teaching, religion must be explained scientifically. The *Divine Principle* states that people should discard outmoded "conventional ideas" about spiritual truth and "should at all costs find the new truth leading them . . . to the new age."[3]

The Transcendental Meditation movement also teaches that the human race is living at a critical crossroads in history. In a speech given in March 1978 and reprinted in a TM publication, Maharishi Mahesh Yogi gives his optimistic views of the New Age:

We in this generation are living in the midst of a fundamental transformation in the trend of time. We are on the threshold of a new age in which enlightenment—pure consciousness or the simplest form of awareness—is increasingly guiding the destiny of human life, thought, action, and behaviour. The age of ignorance is receding, and the sunshine of the Age of Enlightenment is on its way to bring fulfillment to the noblest aspirations of mankind.[4]

The Maharishi has praised modern science because, in his view, it has verified the benefits of Transcendental Meditation. Science has also achieved the capability of nuclear annihilation. However, the TM movement stands ready to "restore meaning and purpose to the scientific age by transforming this dangerous situation into the path of evolution and enlightenment." "His Holiness," the Maharishi, is revered as one who "as long ago as 1975" had, through unceasing efforts, "already brought about the dawn of the Age of Enlightenment, heralding an era characterized by success, prosperity, perfect health, and fulfillment, and freedom from suffering from struggle."[5]

According to the Church Universal and Triumphant, the ascended masters (spiritual teachers of the past) of the Great White Brotherhood have summoned Mark and Elizabeth Prophet to be the messengers of God to release the sacred scriptures of the Aquarian age to the waiting world. Writing from the Ashram of the World Mother in a letter dated "Autumn Equinox, 1977," Guru Ma (Elizabeth Clare Prophet) announced: "The flame of Aquarius is upon us. . . . We see all around us the signs of the end times which Jesus described in chapter twenty-four of the book of Matthew, signifying that the end of the age of Pisces is upon us and the rising sun of a new order of the ages is about to appear."[6]

The Findhorn Foundation on the north coast of Scotland is often cited as a model New Age community. An informational brochure describes the members as "building a new consciousness and a new world." Findhorn is called "a community that inspires and confirms for people that there is a new age upon us."

In an interview published in the *New Age Dawn*, Norman Paulsen, founder of the New Age-oriented Sunburst Communities, describes the dawning of the New Age from the perspective of a seeker who was not satisfied with the intellectual knowledge associated with organized Christianity. "I had to get my hands on God. And see him and know him. I could never be satisfied just to take somebody's word for it. . . . The Aquarian Age is the age of 'I know.' The old age of Pisces says, 'Let's have faith.'"

The expression "New Age religion" is generally associated with those groups having an eclectic or Eastern mystical heritage. Although the label is generally not applied to those groups and movements which I have called aberrant Christian, the concepts of newness, restoration and recovery are crucial to their belief systems as well.

John Robert Stevens, founder and chief apostle of the Church of the Living Word (also called "The Walk"), boasted in a sermon in 1975 that "there is nothing in the world as great as the Walk that God has brought forth."[7] Elsewhere, he predicted that "this Walk . . . will be the largest spiritual move ever to come forth in the history of the Church."[8]

Like so many aberrant Christian groups, the Walk claims to have more truth than any other Christian body. Although they would deny publicly that they sanction extrabiblical revelation, a much-emphasized aspect of their movement involves the notion of "new levels of revelation." Stevens declared, "God has given the apostolic ministry a unique ability to break into new levels in God and then impart them to the people." In the same sermon he continued, "This Walk is ordained to come into tremendous wisdom and revelation about the age to come. . . . This school of the prophets is

. . . loosing the earth; it is loosing another age. I feel that the timing of the age unfolding to us now is something almost given into our hands. We are bringing it forth."[9]

Looking to the East

While it is helpful to recognize the ways in which the various new religious groups describe their unique perspectives on the present age and to understand the implications of those perceived distinctions for both doctrine and practice, it is imperative to ask the larger sociological question: Why the explosion of cults on the American scene at this point in history? Is their emergence in recent years a sociological sign of the times, a spiritual indicator of the times or both?

Before we analyze the ethos of the sixties and seventies and ask how that particular cultural matrix engendered so many expressions of religion, we must remember that America's penchant for religious novelty is not restricted to the past few decades. A historical perspective will reveal this nation's propensity for religious innovation and pluralism. Commenting on what he calls "America's religious fecundity," noted historian Sydney Ahlstrom concludes: "American civilization from the beginning and in each passing century has been continuously marked by extraordinary religious fertility, and continues to exhibit this propensity to the present day."[10]

America has always been predisposed to innovation. The nineteenth century, particularly the period between 1820 and 1860, witnessed the emergence of a host of new sects during a time of great social and religious upheaval. Utopian communal groups like the Shakers and the Oneida Community became as familiar to the American religious landscape as the Mormons, Campbellites and Millerites. European visitors, local townspeople and curious clergy would visit such groups and remark (not always favorably) about their unusual attire, social organization and religious customs.

When we look at the upsurge of new religious movements in the recent past, however, we must conclude that the nature of newness in American religious experience has assumed some truly new dimensions. Religious historian Eldon G. Ernst has noted that "the range of the new in contemporary American religious life and thought has moved beyond the experience of earlier generations. The movement is away from the boundaries of the Judeo-Christian heritage of Western civilization."[11]

What, then, is new about the new religious movements? First, there is the deep imprint of Asian spirituality. To be sure, Eastern mysticism took root in American soil long before the twentieth century. The impact of Eastern religion on mainstream American culture, however, has been very noticeable since the advent of the counterculture of the late 1960s. With its emphasis on inner experience and the achieving of a detached tranquility, Zen Buddhism has been one of the most pervasive influences on the American counterculture and, in turn, on the larger youth culture. Thirty years ago in the United States one might have thought that a *guru* was an exotic animal. Today, because of Zen and other Eastern spiritual disciplines, it is practically a household word.

The most obvious impact of Eastern thinking in North America today is the enormous popularity of Transcendental Meditation. Nearly a million Americans have been initiated into TM. "What McDonald's has done for the hamburger, TM has done for Eastern mysticism. . . . TM has made Eastern mysticism acceptable, fashionable, and desirable to the public by saturating the American consciousness."[12]

Harvard theologian Harvey Cox has written a book whose title, *Turning East*, describes the spiritual sojourn of many young Americans. Why are so many people drawn to Neo-Oriental movements for spiritual enlightenment? According to Cox, "They are looking first of all for friendship and second for a directly felt experience of God and the world. In addition, they seem to be seeking a way out of intellectual and moral confusion, a kind of innocence, or a way of life unmarred by sex stereotypes or technological overkill."[13]

Another significant aspect of the expanding range of newness on the current religious scene is the emphasis on consciousness and the altering of human consciousness. During the sixties, the counterculture and its preoccupation with psychedelic drugs brought "altered states of consciousness," new ways of perceiving reality, to an unprecedented number of young Americans.

The new religious cults of the post-counterculture era offered young people drugless alternatives to the expanded states of consciousness they had experienced via LSD, mescaline and peyote. Drug trips were replaced by spiritual states of rapture induced by chanting, meditation and other forms of spiritual technology.

Truth or Consciousness

Today, consciousness exploration and experimentation remain as central features of the new religious quest. Theodore Roszak, well-known commentator on the counterculture, explains the positive stance taken toward these psychospiritual explorations: "Perhaps that is the greatest discovery which the current religious awakening—taken as a whole—has brought us: a sense of how much bigger and more grandly various religion can be than the narrow fixation upon Belief and Doctrine that has for so long preoccupied the major churches of the West."[14]

The thrust of the new religious groups—whether Eastern mystical, occult or aberrant Christian—is that experience is more important than doctrine, feeling more important than rationality.

Truth, according to many young people today, is not attained by traditional modes of learning but by mystical insight. It can be found by "opening up to cosmic energy," by direct experience with the universe, by pursuing the wisdom of the East. As sociologists Stark and Bainbridge observe, "While the mainline denominations discard their traditional confessions, clash over the ordination of women and homosexuals, and often seem to regard the governance of South Africa as the central religious matter of the day . . . other movements, both sects and cults, are dealing in a far richer expression of the supernatural."[15]

In the new religious and quasi-religious movements, the method is often the message. Across America millions of people are experiencing profound changes in their lives as they pursue "peak experiences," "bliss," "unbounded awareness," "becoming clear" and "cosmic consciousness." There is a preoccupation with self-help techniques designed to create new "inner energy" and "self-actualization." The emphasis on self-discovery has resulted in what some observers are calling "the new narcissism." This turning inward in order to achieve self-realization is accomplished with the assistance of a whole new spiritual technology—techniques for expanding human awareness which include meditation, chanting, Tibetan prayer wheels, body movement and the use of sound vibrations. This emphasis on methodology is the outgrowth of spiritual meaning and self-understanding described by Conway and Siegelman in their book *Snapping:*

> In the early sixties, with the increase in leisure and affluence, the advent of psychedelic drugs and the rediscovery of Eastern thought, Americans set out to explore the underused, often dormant capacities of thought, feeling, imagination, self-expression and relationship that have come to be known as their human potential. In the process, they crossed new thresholds of sensation and discovered the "high," the privileged domain of peak experience attainable through drugs and encounter groups, and meditation. . . . The search was on: for the highest high, the tallest peak, the deepest reach of experience.[16]

Many young Americans during the decade of the sixties were leading lives of ease and emptiness. Disenchanted with the establishment, disoriented by the drug culture and disillusioned with the failure of radical politics, the time was right for the emergence of the new religious movements. In the midst of uncertainty and a massive confusion of values, New Age religion provided a form of security and an unerring map for the youthful searchers.

The 1960s and 1970s, a period of massive upheaval and social change, set the scene for the meteoric rise of the cults. It was the first time in Western cultural history that Eastern metaphysics and the "new consciousness" made a significant impact on our society.

For the Christian, New Age spirituality is intrinsically counterfeit. The goal of Christian worship is not the expansion of consciousness or the experience of self-realization or ego enlightenment. As David Fetcho observes:

There is no question that, from a Biblical vantage, the New Age spirituality represents a pantheistic idolatry, particularly in its exaltation of humanity's alleged divinity. Moreover, we know that whatever ingenious solutions the New Age may come up with will still be in the context of human rebellion against God—simply because they are attempts to undo the results of the curse without confronting its source."[17]

FOUR

Following the Leader

W ho are the people most vulnerable to the new religious movements? Why are so many young people joining cults? What are they seeking? What kinds of needs are aberrant Christian groups filling that more conventional churches are not meeting?

New Age religions and aberrant Christian groups seem to draw the majority of their new recruits from the seventeen-to-twenty-five-year-old age bracket. There are exceptions at both ends of this age range, but, for the most part, cults are populated by young adults. The People's Temple of Jim Jones, with a membership which ranged from small children to senior citizens, was atypical in its age composition when compared with other cults which have emerged since the mid-sixties. Rajneesh's community seemed to attract people at mid-life.

Young people are subject to the inherent vulnerabilities of that ambiguous social status known as adolescence. They experience the dilemmas traditionally associated with that prolonged limbo between childhood and full adulthood and thus find in the cults a resolution to their very real problems. In a society which demands extended and highly specialized training in a context of continuous change and uncertainty, an all-encompassing religious movement provides a moratorium on growing up, a secure environment where decisions about careers, education and starting a family can often be deferred or avoided.

For this reason, cults tend to attract a disproportionate number of young adults who lack self-direction and purpose and who need an external source of authority to provide a framework for their lives. They are people looking for definite answers, clear moral and spiritual guidelines, firm structures. In new religious groups these youths find their needs are met—simple, black-and-white answers; a group structure to help them overcome their insecurity and loneliness; and leaders who manifest absolute conviction and certainty.

In this sense, the new cults can be viewed as escapist alternatives to the complexity of contemporary life, avoidance mechanisms for those unable to cope with their feelings of anxiety, insecurity and isolation. Extremist cults—with their encompassing and encapsulating characteristics—exploit the dependency needs of their members. This is especially true of those groups which are communal in orientation. The members' basic needs—food, housing, clothing, companionship—are provided. In the same way that inmates of prisons and mental hospitals become "institutionally dependent," some members of extremist religious cults exhibit a tendency to surrender their autonomy, their independent decision-making capacity, to the group.

This is not to say that all cult members are weak-willed, insecure or emotionally unstable persons prior to their entry into the group. To be sure, studies of psychiatrists indicate that a significant percentage of converts had major personality problems before they joined a new religious movement. Such groups invariably attract a contingent of the lost and the losers. But so do conventional religious groups.

On the Road to Find Out

People join cults because they hope such groups will fulfill very real, perceived needs. These needs are generated in large part by the changing and confusing society that is America today, and reflect a spiritual vacuum in what many believe is rapidly becoming a post-Christian era. New Age groups mirror their culture; they promise simplistic solutions to the discontinuities of that culture. As Ethel Romm so astutely observes:

In looking-glass language, the new panaceas promise unity in a fractured society, peace in a warring society, liberation in a repressed society, balance in a shaken society, purity in a polluted society, goodness in a corrupt society, growth in a constricting society, psychic powers in an overbearing society, health in a sick society, relaxation in a tense society, happiness in a discontented society, awareness in a numb society, spirituality in a materialistic society.[1]

In an age of industrialization, secularization, materialism and prolonged adolescence, many young people are attempting to resolve inner conflict by the proverbial search for one's identity. In an era of dislocation and uncertainty, the new cultic groups give the individual a location, or what Martin Marty calls a "sense of demarcation."[2] Such groups provide a clear sense of who is inside and who is outside the circle of true believers. "One knows *exactly* what to expect of Baba-lovers, followers of the Reverend Sun Myung Moon, or Hare Krishna chanters—there are no surprises. That is how the members want it; therein is much of the appeal, in an age of identity diffusion and absence of demarcational lines in society and most of its faiths."[3]

Ultimately, the quest for identity involves the quest for meaning, a spiritual search. Most young people who become a part of New

Age groups have very nominal religious backgrounds. Some have had no formal religious affiliation whatsoever. Those having a conventional religious background usually describe it negatively: their spiritual or fellowship needs were unmet; their church or synagogue did not supply the answers to life's major questions.

Not only are they involved in a genuine spiritual search, but young people who are highly vulnerable to cultic appeals are also usually very idealistic. They have been frustrated in earlier attempts to bring about positive social change and have become disillusioned. Such individuals—basically religious in orientation while at the same time desirous of making the world a better place—are prime targets for new movements like the Unification Church. A Moonie recruitment poster suggests: "If you want to change this world and are longing to find the way . . . you are the person who should hear the Divine Principle Seminar!"

The Unification Church has a rather elaborate theological system outlined in its own bible, the *Divine Principle*. Many people engaged in a serious spiritual search find that Unification theology "makes sense" and is intellectually satisfying. "It all seemed so logical," ex-members frequently explain as they reflect on their initial attraction to the Moonies. This notion is also illustrated in a personal testimony published in a Unification Church periodical:

All the proof that I have ever needed about this being the right thing has been laid out right in front of me since the first day I came. The Principle not only makes sense, it covers everything. No matter what situation I find by following the Principle, it's impossible to really go wrong.[4]

All in the Family
Perhaps an even stronger attraction of the cults is the sense of family which they convey. A large sign just inside the entrance of a Unification Church center in a major American city proclaims, "Welcome Home!" Significantly, one of the early names of the Unification Church was "The Unified Family." Even today,

members informally refer to their group as "the Family." A Unificationist publication states: "More than ever we are a Family, serving each other as daughters and sons, brothers and sisters, mothers and fathers under Our True Parents [Mr. Moon and his wife]."[5]

The new religious movements of the 1980s have supplied a new kind of family to searching, vulnerable young adults. These groups capitalize on feelings of belonging and fraternity. Some of the young people who are drawn to the cults come from broken homes or situations where communication with parents was strained or completely absent. Others come from very affluent homes where overt love and care were minimal. As one former cult member put it, "My parents had never cared where I was, and it was really neat to think that someone actually might be worried about me."

The new cults offer young people a context where they are accepted, cared for, loved, fed and housed, and made to feel important. This affirmation, this sense of being loved, was the main attraction for a young woman who joined an aberrant Christian group known simply as Faith Tabernacle:

You really felt like a part of a large family. When you finally met Pastor, you fell in love with her at once. Everything about her personality was attractive. She treated you like you were really special. Most of the young people affectionately called her "Mother." The newcomers soon adopted that term also because she treated you like you were her own child. This woman [Mrs. Daries] was constantly saying, "I love you." I know now that my parents loved me, but they didn't know how to demonstrate it.

It is instructive that sect leaders are often addressed in parental terms: "Father" David (of the Family of Love), "Grandfather" Paulsen (of Sunburst Communities), "Father" Moon (of the Unification Church), "Dad" Jones (of the People's Temple). The followers of Moon and his wife ("Mother") sometimes sign letters, "in the Name of Our True Parents."

The imagery of the family is strong in the cults. The word *family* occurs in the names of several prominent groups: the Unified Family, the Love Family, the Christ Family, the Family of Love (formerly known as the Children of God) and the Manson Family. These "spiritual" families replace the members' natural families. Biological parents are often castigated, ignored or viewed as tools of Satan. Thus while exploiting the human desire to be part of a familial group, the cults undermine the God-ordained social institution of the family by substituting their own spiritualized versions.

Truth and the Need to Belong
Another reason people are attracted to cults and deviant Christian groups is the desire for absolutist leadership. As Martin Marty correctly notes, this type of orientation can lead to narrow-mindedness: "The religious impulse calls people from the distractions of a random world and helps them make sense of things. Religion could be called 'Meaning and Belonging, Incorporated'; when those who find meaning around the same vision or the same master link up, they can become dangerously intolerant."[6]

The quest for spiritual fulfillment often involves a search for truth via mystical insight. Truth, according to many New Age gurus, "is found in populist, homespun wisdom, in anti-universities, in direct experience with the cosmos, in meditation, in chants, in drugs, in sensory deprivation, in sensitivity to the messages of the intuitive right hemisphere of the brain."[7] Immediate experience is given primacy over doctrinal belief. The emphasis is on the spontaneous rather than the structured. The message emanating from the counterculture and beamed at today's youthful searchers is: "Pursue a sense of mystery and fantasy, embrace the occult, meditate, unlock the truth that is in you."[8] Truth, according to this perspective, is attainable by anyone through an inner light or by rediscovering the mysteries of the ancients.

This view runs counter to what Jesus explicitly taught: "If you hold to my teaching, you are really my disciples. Then you will know the truth, and the truth will set you free" (Jn 8:31-32). For the Christian, ultimate truth is the person, the word and the work of Jesus Christ.

Another attraction of the cults is the sense of community they provide. American society, while enjoying the benefits of technology, has been called a "lonely crowd." The fragmenting effects of our urbanized, supermarket society are familiar to us all. It is the sense of integration, the knowledge of being part of a nationwide or worldwide network, the sense of a commonly shared mission which melds the convert to the cult. An ex-Moonie writing in *The Harvard Crimson* put it this way:

Moon requires his followers to sacrifice everything for the cause. All possessions and monies are given to the church and one's family, friends and future plans are all forsaken. In exchange for these sacrifices Moon provides a strong, supportive community, a powerful father figure, the basic necessities of life and eternal salvation. With these assets, the movement is growing at a tremendous rate.[9]

At the heart of the upsurge in new religious movements is what Romm terms "the yearning of seekers for a genuine community to belong to, the kind of fellowship long since absent from our starched churches."[10]

As I have already indicated, the most vulnerable age group for cult recruitment is the immediate post-high-school population. Many in this group are on the move, part of the backpack subculture, when they first encounter the cults. Frequently they are introduced to cultic religion in California, literally the end of the line for our highly mobile youth culture. These "new migrants" are drawn to California, the spawning ground for so many of the new religions, because they are disillusioned with life "back home" and are attracted to the state's hospitable environment and reputation for openness. Many are, in the apt description of Dr. Margaret Singer, "between affiliations." They reside in those vulnerable periods between high school and college, between college and a job, or between careers or marriages.

Studies show that many young people who join cults are experiencing some form of personal crisis when first approached. They are down on their luck, depressed, confused, lacking a sense of direction. Research involving 237 members of the Unification Church, for example, revealed that nearly two-thirds of the respondents had serious emotional or drug-related problems prior to joining the Moonies.[11] Others are merely curious or spiritually hungry—or both.

Sociologically, it is interesting that most adherents of the new religious movements are from the middle and upper-middle social classes. "To put it simply, successful cults may skim more of the cream of society than the dregs."[12] This is a departure from historical precedent; sects have traditionally drawn their members from the disadvantaged classes, from those on the fringes of society. People who are into Lifespring or who have joined the ranks of the Hare Krishnas are more likely to come from suburban Los Angeles than from rural Appalachia.

Aberrant Christian groups tend to obtain a considerable number of their adherents from more conventional evangelical churches. Members of such groups typically cite their disenchantment with standard evangelical churches which, according to the defectors, lack power and true spirituality.

FIVE

False Prophets and True Believers

Messianic movements are not confined to the last few decades of human history. There have always been those "true believers," possessing fanatical faiths and incredible dedication, who have been willing to yield their identity to a group and sacrifice their lives for a holy cause. Convinced that they are in possession of some irresistible power and are the sole repositories of "the truth," zealots of both political and religious causes have time and again engaged in the transcendental game of follow the leader.

As Eric Hoffer and others have pointed out, mass movements need charismatic leaders to evoke enthusiasm, direct human energies, provide spiritual and psychic sustenance, and command the sense of loyalty and self-sacrifice typical of such movements. "Once the stage is set, the presence of an outstanding leader is indispensable. Without him there will be no movement."[1]

Rigid, charismatic, authoritarian leadership is the keystone of most all cultic movements. The qualities of messianic leadership, according to Hoffer, include "audacity, fanatical faith in a holy cause, an awareness of the importance of a close-knit collectivity, and, above all, the ability to evoke to fervent devotion in a group of able lieutenants."[2] Such a leader exudes certitude, self-confidence and self-importance. He or she must be able to kindle and fan a sense of hope and trust within the ranks of the faithful.

Charisma and Crisis

Charisma, according to *Webster's New Collegiate Dictionary*, is "a quality of extraordinary spiritual power attributed to a person capable of eliciting popular support in the direction of human affairs."

In order to fully understand the dynamics of the new religious movements, the crucial significance of charisma—the unusual capacity to influence others—must be underscored. Concepts such as "mind control" and "brainwashing," while colorfully descriptive categories, are sometimes vague and imprecise labels when applied to cultic behavior. The notion of charismatic influence, on the other hand, focuses on the visible dimensions of leadership and its effects on the lives of followers.

Charismatic persons "usually rise to prominence during times of intense social strife, or when shifting social mores leave groups of people without a stable set of beliefs in which they can feel secure."[3] The United States has been undergoing a massive cultural shift which has predisposed our nation to the influx of new mysticisms and new messiahs. The gurus and religious entrepreneurs have taken full advantage of that cultural/spiritual predisposition. As Professor K. J. Ratnam explains, "They are often persons who succeed more than others in exploiting the situation around them. They know what their people feel most strongly about or can be made to feel strongly about. In a way, they are not 'picked' by their people; it is the other way round."[4]

Jim Jones was the epitome of a charismatic leader. His charm and personal magnetism made him appealing to people of diverse backgrounds and diverse age groups. He fashioned his utopian socialist experiment from readily available human and ideological resources. He could inspire hope and create community. He manipulated public officials as well as his obedient followers. Like all false prophets, he preached his own version of salvation and directed that message at very vulnerable people. Exemplifying the ultimate form of charismatic control, he subverted wills, vandalized souls and demanded lives.

> People came to Jim Jones because he promised to help them fulfill needs and aspirations which we denied in our society, because he offered them ordered intimacy, an end to doubt and thought, and a perfect unalloyed way of thinking and being. They stayed because he helped them pretend they did not know that he was lying to himself and to them, because they chose to make his delusions theirs. They died not because they were brainwashed, but because they felt they had gone too far to come back or because the leader to whom they consigned their will ordered them to be murdered.[5]

Ironically, charismatic prophets have as much need for followers as followers have need for a leader. Phil Tracy describes this strangely symbiotic relationship between Jim Jones and his congregation:

> Step by step Jones and his fateful flock kept upping their dependence on each other. The more his followers praised him, the greater were Jones's claims of power: a deadly two-step dance. By the time Jones "revealed" himself, they were primed to accept him as their messiah, the one who would lead them out of the treacherous, blindly evil world he had created inside their heads. . . . Jones achieved a degree of power rarely felt by mortal men. No one dared question his word. In the eyes of his flock, he was omnipotent.[6]

Worship, Idolatry and Leaders

Although Jones often masqueraded as a "fundamentalist" Christian, he, in fact, preached another Jesus, another gospel. Later in his ecclesiastical career he even claimed to be a manifestation of the deity. He convinced his congregation that he was God. As Mel White relates, Jones replaced the God of the Bible with Jim Jones:

Wayne Pietila, who joined the cult as a youngster, remembers that Jones seemed gradually to see himself as God's replacement. "Jim Jones was like a father to me," he remembers. "I could go to him when I had problems, talk to him, and he always understood. . . But as the years went by, he became colder to the individual needs of the people and started wanting himself put upon a pedestal like God.

"In 1973 he actually came out and said he wanted to be called *Father*, and he wanted us to pray to him. He wanted us to carry around his picture in our wallets."[7]

An ex-Moonie describes the adoration felt for his leader: "We would conjure up his image in our minds. I knew his face better than I knew my own. . . . I knew his face so well and I loved him so much! I thought about him all the time!"[8] Later this same young woman struggled with her emotions regarding Moon as she was leaving the movement: "I had a locket with Moon's picture in it, and on the first night of the deprogramming, I very quietly slid the picture out of the locket and swallowed it. I didn't want anything done to that photograph. . . . For about a month after leaving the movement I still couldn't look at a picture of Moon . . . because I had loved him so much."[9]

One former member of the People's Temple sums up the feeling of so many true believers who have been spiritually seduced by false prophets: "I needed a sort of God-figure or an authority figure in my life, so I think I just replaced Jesus Christ with Jim Jones."[10] This self-proclaimed savior had his Jonestown faithful repeat what were called "the three gratitudes": "Thanks, Dad, for bringing us here, thanks for the food, thanks for the weather."

An ex-follower of "The Perfect Master," Guru Maharaj Ji, illustrates this principle common to many of the newer sects—the deification of a particular, highly imperfect human being:

You are allowed access to a real experience of transcendance [sic]. There is a great emotional tie to your fellow devotees and to your Guru—your Guru, being the center stage of everything you do, becomes omnipresent. Everything is ascribed to him. He is positively supernatural after a while. . . . That feeling of love, of community. The certainty that you are submitting to God incarnate.[11]

Whether it involves the worship of false prophets or the bowing down to false gods, the Bible calls such behavior idolatry. Scripture records an event when even an angel of God refused to receive the worship of a human. "I, John, am the one who heard and saw these things. And when I had heard and seen them, I fell down to worship at the feet of the angel who had been showing them to me. But he said to me, 'Do not do it! I am a fellow servant with you and with your brothers the prophets and of all who keep the words of this book. Worship God!' " (Rev 22:8-9).

The more idolatrous Jones became, the more he sank into madness. Power always corrupts except when it is exercised in perfection; by and in Jesus Christ. Jones thought he was God; Jesus was. It is striking that Jesus, though worthy Himself of worship, always pointed away from Himself to his Father. Isolated in a rain forest of a distant land, Jones more and more pointed to himself. Arrogance and idolatry are of a piece, and they always end in disaster and death.[12]

In another time and another place, sermons were preached in churches extolling yet another "long-promised savior": "Adolf Hitler is the voice of Jesus Christ, who desired to become flesh and blood of the German people and did become flesh and blood." In day nurseries, children repeated this prayer:

Führer, my Führer, by God given to me,
Defend and protect me as long as may be.

Thou'st Germany rescued from her deepest need;
I render thee thanks who dost daily me feed.
Stay by me forever, or desperate my plight.
Führer, my Führer, my faith, my light,
Hail, my Führer![13]

A god in the flesh is easier for some people to believe in.

While he has not been elevated to messianic or deity status, John Robert Stevens was given a place of extraordinary power and prominence by his followers in the Church of the Living Word. "Apostle" Stevens had an exalted view of himself and his ministry: "I do not believe that my ministry will go forth as much as the spiritual force will pull men to me to be taught. Wherever I am, men will be drawn. They have to come for what God has ordained to complete their ministry."[14]

Stevens also placed a strong emphasis on authority and subjection—being in submission to the "Apostle" and his "apostolic company": "Those who are submissive will accept a word of authority over them, even when that word is wrong. . . . If the Lord has revealed the authority over you, you can be submissive, even when the authority deviates from the will of God. In other words, you can receive some wrong words of direction and still be a winner."[15]

It is reported by ex-members of the Walk that one pastor in the movement repeatedly made the remark, "I would follow Brother Stevens to hell, and God would honor me for it because of my submission!"

In 1971 a series of prophecies were received supposedly pointing to Stevens's role as God's apocalyptic prophet and "Apostle of Apostles." The transcribed text of the prophecies includes the following statement: "I have chosen you to walk as a leader, to take My people in this generation into the Kingdom of God. The heavens and earth are now resting upon your shoulders that you shall lead the people of God into their final destiny of walking in the Kingdom of God."[16]

In a June 1986 sermon, Donald Barnett, pastor of Seattle's controversial Community Chapel, used military imagery to describe his role as commander-in-chief of that segment of God's army:

I have always wanted an army under me that would do what I ask—just like that. Not for me. A general never fights for himself. . . . I have wanted for Him to have a people that would follow. . . . But I am commander of this army. . . . I am asking for a new submission to your pastor. . . . We're going to go through a battle and you're going to see that those who have brought themselves to the place of discipline and submission, who are really and truly behind their pastor, are going to be the people who are behind God. . . . I know that God wants you to do what I ask you to do and I know that if you don't, you are going against God Himself.

Eleanor Daries is the charismatic "Pastor" of Faith Tabernacle, formerly located in Southern California. She is charismatic in both theology and personality. Mrs. Daries is the "Oracle of God," a feminine "Moses" leading her people into the land of holiness. Like all cult leaders, she demands blind obedience and total loyalty. She requires members of her largely communal congregation to write letters and statements pledging their devotion to her. Each letter would start or conclude with a statement that it was written of the writer's own volition, and if the writer ever said otherwise he would be guilty of lying.

Such letters also contained statements implying that all money given to the church or to Mrs. Daries was given as a "freewill offering." Members had to promise that they would never, under any circumstances, request that any of the money be returned—even if they should become "reprobate" and leave the church. According to one such reprobate, "These letters were sent to her and returned to us until we got the wording exactly right. Then she would accept them." Mrs. Daries keeps these letters and other pertinent information in several large files in her house. They are used for purposes of intimidation and control.

A former member of Faith Tabernacle describes Pastor Daries

as an attractive, middle-aged woman with a disarming personality: I came to look up to her and admire her, almost in a fanatical way. She had a fantastic personality that drew people like a magnet. Once under her power, she could make you believe almost anything. I loved her very much, and the desire to have her return that love and friendship was so strong that I was willing to do almost anything to get it. She used this knowledge to control me for a long time—never quite letting me close enough to satisfy me, yet always holding satisfaction before me as a hope, as one would hold bait before an animal.

The Call of the Prophet

What motivates a false prophetess, a misguided messiah, or a self-appointed apostle? "The Messiah business has many advantages. You don't need academic training or degrees. No financial investment is necessary, and the financial rewards are unreal. No mortal work is more prestigious. Even an unexalted past is no deterrent."[17]

Cult leaders are typically engaged in what they are doing for one or more of the following reasons. First, they are able to exercise power over people. The ability to manipulate and control other people's lives can be very satisfying to one's ego. It is a phenomenon not restricted to cults, as anyone familiar with human behavior can attest. Second, they are in it for the money. Financial aggrandizement is a common hallmark of cultic movements and quasi-religious self-improvement organizations. Third, cult leaders may sincerely believe what they preach. They may honestly believe that the teachings of their group are the answer to the world's problems. Hitler, no doubt, believed his own delusions.

The question is often asked: "Could the experience of Nazi Germany be repeated?" Dusty Sklar sees parallels between what happened in Germany before and after World War 2 and what is developing on the contemporary cult scene today:

Then, as now, people put their trust in a single man, revered him as a saint, loved him like a father. They were prepared to follow him into the bowels of Hell. Hitler was said to have had a magnetic personality, but this is hardly necessary, nor was he seen in this light by some of those who were immune to his message. There are leaders preaching to multitudes today who have no discernible power to attract, other than the will of people to believe in them. And no matter how ridiculous the edicts handed down from on high—perhaps *because* they are ridiculous—believers are eager to justify and rationalize.[18]

Christ warned us that during the end times there would be an increase in the number of false prophets: "At that time if anyone says to you, 'Look, here is the Christ!' or, 'There he is!' do not believe it. For false Christs and false prophets will appear and perform great signs and miracles to deceive even the elect—if that were possible. See, I have told you ahead of time" (Mt 22:23-25).

SIX

A Firm Hold: The Ties That Bind

Donna was introduced to the Faith Tabernacle commune at a low point in her life. After graduating from a Christian college, she was dissatisfied with her job and had just experienced a broken engagement. She went with some friends to a Sunday service at Faith Tabernacle (FT). The church was attractively built and looked clean and neat. Donna was impressed by the friendliness of the people. "As a visitor, I was surrounded by friendly people eager to make me feel welcome, at home, and at ease. I was impressed by the seriousness with which these people took their religion.

"After the service everyone seemed so happy and friendly and wanted to meet me. I hadn't had that much attention in a long time and secretly enjoyed it. They made you feel that you must really be a very attractive and interesting person to merit such attention. You would be invited to lunch where you would hear members of the group talk about all the fun they had doing things together. Everyone would be laughing and talking and you would have a wonderful afternoon. You were told many times how wonderful the leader was, and you would begin to feel a real urge to meet this person whom everyone talked so much about."

Donna began to attend services with regularity. "Each week you would be welcomed by people who remembered your name, and they would be anxious to tell you of the exciting and wonderful things the group had done that past week. You began to think you were really missing something because you hadn't been a part of the activity. They would tell you that if you didn't have transportation [from Los Angeles] they would even offer to come and get you and take you home again. If you missed a service, one of your new friends would call to say they missed you and wondered if you were sick."

A few months later Donna quit her job and moved into a singles' "dorm" at the commune. "I shipped all my books and most of my possessions to my parents and gave everything I had of monetary value to the Pastor [Mrs. Daries] as a sign of submission to her authority. I had only met 'Pastor' a couple of times, but she had totally wound me around her finger. I adored her and was ready to do anything in hopes of some day being like her. She was everything I had never been. I felt I was a total failure as a person. 'Pastor' constantly glowed. You could almost feel the presence of her personality before you even saw her. Everything came alive when she entered the room. She was a perfect lady, graceful, pretty, gracious, having the carriage and manner more associated with royalty or nobility than with a pastor. She had the ability to make you feel at ease at once, and she let you know she was interested in you as a person and cared about you. When she laughed or smiled it was so contagious it could bring you out of any gloom. She radiated life and vitality, was totally feminine, and at the same time managed to make her authority and strength felt. One felt both awed and drawn to her."

Donna had some personality problems when she joined Faith Tabernacle. The leaders reassured her that many of the members had faced similar problems and had found answers through the discipline and self-sacrifice found at the commune. "They insisted that the answer to life lay in renouncing self and all earthly ties to family, friends, and possessions, and by giving oneself entirely to serving God through the special mission of the commune.

"For a while everything about the commune was a dream come true. I got an interesting job, and the rest of my time was planned for me. There was no need to think—that was all done for me by the group. I was escaping responsibility and the pressures it brought. I could again be a child, joining the others in calling the Pastor 'Mother' and in mentally thinking of myself as a child in a family—being loved, protected and cared for with very little to do in return.

"This type of life continued for about two years. By then I was convinced I had found the real answer to life. I was having more fun than I had ever had in my life, I seemed to be making progress toward my goals, and I was part of a group that was really 'doing things' for God."

When Donna started dating a young man in the group, she began to see the dark underside of Faith Tabernacle. "As with most things, nothing was ever said initially about my dating that one could put a finger on, but I soon realized I was losing the approval I had had and gaining much disapproval. I had heard many sermons in FT on how terrible marriage was, but I hadn't listened much. Now the pressure was really on, and I felt it from every side."

In the opinion of ex-members of Faith Tabernacle, the leader, Mrs. Daries, hated men. Perhaps this hatred was the result of two apparently unhappy marriages. "She taught that women should rule everything, and that men didn't have any brains and weren't good for anything except to father children. While marriage was not openly condemned, it was greatly discouraged, and celibacy was loudly proclaimed to be much holier."

This attitude was very much in evidence during the weeks before Donna's wedding. "I was called to special meetings where I was told how terrible my fiancé was—that he couldn't manage money, that he never kept himself or his clothes or his room clean, and that I would have a terrible time keeping house for him. I was constantly told that I was throwing away the 'precious call of God on my life' for a man, and that all I wanted was filthy sex and lust. I was told many horrible things about his mother, a woman I didn't really know, until I thoroughly hated her.

"I had to sign a pledge—under pressure—that I would remain loyal to the group even if he or his family were not, although this did not include a pledge to divorce him, as he was later led to believe. I thought that my fiancé had to sign a similar vow, and I was told that he would leave me if I ever said anything against the group."

Donna was asked to attend secret night meetings. At these gatherings, the inner core members and leaders subjected her to various types of "discipline"—usually a combination of public humiliation and interrogation. "Feeling the scorn and contempt of the group and being frozen out of the activities I so enjoyed were hard to take. I often left these meetings with my emotions ripped completely to shreds and became physically sick. Yet I was expected to go to work the next day as if nothing had happened. I wanted out of the group at this point, but I had signed a lot of loyalty vows and getting out wasn't so easy—especially when you actually believed that to break those vows might really bring on God's wrath and anger.

"In an attempt to destroy my pride—which was presented as an ugly sin—I continued to submit to public humiliations. After many such sessions, the Pastor evidently decided that I could not be broken in this way and the tactics changed. The wedding took place and I was sure everything would now work out."

Donna was restored to favor in the group and began receiving special attention. "Evidently Pastor had decided my time as a novice was over, and that in order to keep me and use me for her purposes, it was time to train me for a position of leadership. At first I thought it was a great honor to be thus singled out. In reality, it turned out to be a trap. I soon discovered that the deeper one got involved in the behind-the-scenes activities of the group, the harder it was to get out. It was like walking a tightrope. I knew I was being moved like a puppet on a string, but to reveal my feelings or to refuse to cooperate would have meant the end of my marriage. I could have left at any time, but I would have left alone and with only the clothes on my back because the leaders had successfully blocked all communication between my husband and me. They had also instilled in each of us a mutual fear that the other would either inform or leave. As a result, we seldom spoke to each other at all. We were married and lived in the same house, but we didn't even know each other.

"Mrs. Daries counted on my desire to keep my husband and used the fear of losing him as a tool to keep me under her control. While at first I accepted the honor of the training program, I was quick to see through it and had no intention of becoming the kind of robot I saw in the other leaders. For a while I played the political game to get to the top, but as I saw more and more of what was going on, I resolved to find the way out. This meant playing their game as long as necessary until I could find an exit for myself and my husband. I began to plan my strategy. What resulted was a psychological battle between the strategy used by the Pastor and the one used by me. Had I known it would take three years to find the escape, I probably would have left my husband and gotten out alone. But I firmly believed that if I played my cards right, I could win sooner than that."

The Mechanisms of Control
What Donna discovered and experienced during those three years was an almost unbelievable system of fear, harsh discipline, power politics, Gestapolike tactics and an incredibly distorted version of

evangelical Christianity. The mechanisms of control employed by the group—based largely on fear and intimidation—are as textbook-typical of cultic activity as can be found anywhere.

Like other extremist cults, Faith Tabernacle exhibited signs of great paranoia. The security system was elaborate, and one had to be a member for several years before the subtle aspects of it were truly noticeable. "To the novice it simply appeared to be a type of protection which merely demonstrated the concern of the older members for the new member's safety. If a woman used a public telephone to make a call, one of the men would always go with her. You never thought of this as a spy system, for the man would casually say, 'Mind if I go along? It really isn't safe for you to be alone around here.' It never entered my head that everything I said and did was reported to the leaders. I didn't even mind that I had to always tell someone even if I went to the store. I thought it was neat that somebody cared!

"The security system had two purposes. For one thing, the leader was extremely paranoid and was sure that people were out to get her. She had to have all dishes sterilized. She drank only carefully sterilized water. She seemed to have an abnormal fear of germs and of being poisoned. She also lived in great fear of being shot or stabbed and constantly had a bodyguard around her.

"The other purpose of the guard system was to keep track of the persons in the commune and to see that no one escaped or in any way got a chance to organize a mutiny. The church compound itself was fenced in with a high, woven-wire fence. To an outsider it looked mainly ornamental, but every inch of it was bugged. No one could enter or leave without the guards knowing it. For a while the large gates were kept locked during services, but later the sheriff made them leave it open. The gate had a combination lock, and the combination was changed frequently. All cupboards in the building had similar combination locks, and only a few people knew these combinations. These too were frequently changed."

Members of the church were carefully trained to "size up" visitors and prospective recruits. An elaborate system of written and oral reports was developed in order to keep tabs on visitors, all of whom were given a friendly mini-interview upon arrival. Someone known to come from a church which was "unfriendly" to the group or someone considered "dangerous" was put under guard at once. Potential members were carefully "ushered" to specific seats, and during the service their reactions were carefully observed and mentally recorded for use in written reports prepared later. All of this appeared to be random and casual, and no one suspected that it was carefully engineered. Likely prospects were then invited to dinner.

According to Donna, guards stood near the doors at all services. "No one ever entered the compound without their knowledge. If a stranger came onto the compound, the guards 'just happened' to be there and would very casually go up to the person and inquire if they could help. They managed to get rid of undesirables. While this was generally done in a friendly manner, they were quite capable of bodily getting rid of someone if necessary."

New members were at first totally unaware of the elaborate reporting system at FT. Eventually, they were introduced to the reporting procedures at carefully planned training sessions. The trainee was warned about the dangers of "leaking" certain information. Great care was taken to impress the trainees with the seriousness of their responsibility to the group. They would have already signed many solemn vows of loyalty and been warned of swift and sure divine wrath should they take things lightly or fail in the responsibility given them. Training was always done "under guard" so that trainees knew how to play their role well before they were ever asked to play it alone. Success in one area would eventually lead to training in another.

Control of group members was accomplished through the use of a complex system of peer and psychological pressure. A member achieved status in the group by informing on others. One of the first lessons learned by a novice was the importance of carefully observing the conduct of other members. "In this way if your roommate slipped and sinned, she could be corrected and wouldn't go to hell. The way it was presented made you feel that you were really helping someone by informing on them and that everyone wanted this help so that they could grow up and become closer to God.

"After you had been there a while, you also learned that if you were closely associated with a person and something was found out about them that you had not reported, you were likely to be under discipline for not doing so. The result was that everybody watched everyone else and cut the other guy's throat in order to save his own neck. Also, in the context of an extremely emotional service, people could be pressured into confessing almost anything. It often became a contest to see who could confess the most. This information was literally stored away and used as a whip if the person later failed to conform."

It was two years after having joined the group that Donna became aware of the heavy disciplinary action employed in the organization. "Until then I was treated much like a child, with correction always being administered gently and carefully and in such a way as to make me feel people were really concerned about helping me to become a better person. The first time I encountered a real discipline session, I was told that this was a very serious matter; if I didn't follow instructions I must leave the meeting as one too 'young' to be trusted. I was then told to pray a prayer and make a vow, calling all kinds of divine punishment on my head if I breathed one word of what happened. I was scared stiff.

"A Japanese boy was then made to stand and undergo interrogation for about an hour. No matter what he answered he was cut down. I watched this strong young man become a sobbing blob of nothing. Actually, this was relatively minor discipline compared to what I was later to witness.

"The leaders seemed to make great use of the psychological effects of little sleep. Most meetings were called in the middle of the night, with no previous warning. When you went you had no idea if the 'victim' was you or someone else. The darkness, combined with the bizarre ways of doing things, added fear and mystery to the proceedings.

"On another occasion we had been at church until very late one night. We were told to leave the main building and go to another building across the compound. Emotions were already at a very high pitch. Upon entering the dimly lit building, we were greeted by an overpowering stench. As our eyes grew accustomed to the dark, we could see tables of rotten food covered with flies and insects. Along the dimly lit walls were hung grotesque pictures depicting every conceivable horror—pictures of violence, people on drugs, pornography. In the background several of the leaders were singing in an eerie voice, 'Come and dine, come and dine, the devil's calling, come and dine.' Pastor then yelled at us, 'This is the type of banquet you want; this is what you choose instead of God's banquet.'

"I felt nauseated, but there was no escape from the crowded room. No one could be sure that we would not be forced to eat the stuff in front of us as punishment for our sins. When we finally got out, we stumbled home weak and sick, only to be called from our beds one hour later and told to come back to church. There, in another small, dimly lit room, the leader appeared in a white robe. In a few minutes one of the members who had broken some rules was dragged out of the restroom, where she had been locked in for some time. She had been dressed like a witch. While she stood in front of everyone, a list of her sins was read for all to hear. (I later learned that this same woman had been threatened with being stripped publicly and smeared with dung.) Her husband had also been through hours of torture, and before that night was over, I saw him groveling on the floor on his stomach like an animal, begging for mercy. On another occasion he was forced to go home after an eight-hour day of hard physical labor and dig up his back yard all night while others in the group jeered at him.

"One night I stood for two hours while group members recounted all the things that were wrong with me. Everyone tried to outdo the other in ripping me apart in the hope of escaping a similar fate themselves. At one meeting two little kids were forced to stand before everyone and describe how they had masturbated. At another meeting a girl got spit on.

"At all of these sessions the emotional pitch reached such explosive proportions it was terrifying. The same group of individuals was never present at any two meetings, and everyone was always made to take vows of secrecy. This meant that my husband and I were seldom at the same meeting, and I never knew how many he had been exposed to. Since no communication was allowed, I never knew what or how much he knew. This lack of communication, combined with the surveillance system, was a very effective tool in keeping people from getting out.

"Most individual activities were discouraged or forbidden. The social times and dating activities were carefully controlled. My husband and I only managed to have a little time alone together once or twice before we were engaged. We had about an hour together the night he gave me my engagement ring.

"I received a lot of pleasure from visiting the museum in the planetarium. This was an outlet for me and I loved it. One time I was planning to take a couple of girls with me there and I was told, 'You can't witness there, so you can't go.' We didn't read newspapers, and magazines were strictly forbidden as well as TV. I was made to quit reading *Time* magazine. You had to turn your mind off.

"Pastor was constantly surrounded by an aura of mystery. No one ever knew where she was or why she was gone. You never knew when she would appear for a service, or if she would show up at all. No one was allowed in her office at church unless summoned, and even then you entered under guard. This was to protect her privacy we were told. You were expected to buy her expensive gifts on every conceivable occasion as a sign of love and loyalty."

Binding the Spirit

The elements of control and intimidation in this narrative of Donna's experience at Faith Tabernacle are present, in varying degrees, in dozens of other extremist cults. The parallels to the People's Temple are striking:

Demonstrations of loyalty were required continually. Jones introduced all-night sessions during which commission members were ordered to stand in the middle of a circle while their friends and loved ones barraged them with personal criticism. Next, they were informed that their marriages and sexual partnerships were corrupt vestiges of the bourgeois order. . . . Spying was systematized. Jones announced that government agents were trying to penetrate the planning commission, and that thereafter each member should be prepared to inform him as to the actions and statements of any other member. Within a matter of months it was part of the daily routine for . . . members to report on the conversations, attitudes, behavior and personal life of all the other members with whom they had contact. . . . During "self-criticism sessions" Jones would have commission members reveal intimacies they had shared with each other. . . . Any personality quirk . . . was used to ridicule, humiliate or punish whoever had displayed it.[1]

Like Faith Tabernacle, Jones had guards protecting entrances. As with Mrs. Daries's followers, Jones's congregation developed a strong sense of loyalty to and trust in their pastor. As Mel White states, "A part of that trust is a willingness to suffer punishment at the hands of the leader."[2] Jones was known to sometimes inflict mental torture and physical punishment on erring members.

We have described the primary control mechanisms which function to hold members—spiritually and psychologically—to cult groups. Sensory deprivation (especially sleep); the severing of all familiar social support systems (old friends, family, former church ties); removal to a highly structured environment where all aspects of one's life are controlled; indoctrination by an exclusivistic group possessing "the truth"; limited access to outside stimulation; diminished ability to think for oneself; the use of fear and intimidation—these are the ties that bind the spirit and cripple the mind.

SEVEN

A Web of Error

A comprehensive analysis of cultic phenomena must include historical, cultural, psychological and sociological dimensions. These academic disciplines have many insights to offer the serious student of the new religious movements. Because of their very nature, however, these approaches fail to deal with the theological and spiritual issues which are at the heart of all false religions. Secular sociologists and psychologists would never label any religion "false," since that represents a value judgment. Behavioral scientists are concerned only with the facts, with empirical data and the theories which assist in explaining those data.

The Christian, however, recognizes that until we examine cult practices in a context of human fallenness, until we identify the web of error that characterizes all groups which depart from the base line of truth found in the Bible, we have only partially understood the dynamics of the new religious groups. "As long as the secular analysts ignore God's consistent proclamation that humanity is fallen and living in alienation from God and is in need of reconciliation through the only reigning Lord, Jesus Christ, they will continue to put band aids on broken arms."[1]

Cultic belief systems range from the fairly simple statement of faith (the "charter") employed by the Church of Armageddon (The Love Family) to the well-developed, rather sophisticated Unification theology associated with the Moonies. Many of the Eastern mystical groups have no formal doctrine and are determinedly nonintellectual in orientation. Eastern religionists "travel light" intellectually, as Martin Marty has observed. "It is not for ideas that one goes to Americanized Asian faiths; of dogma there has been plenty in the West, say those open to conversion."[2]

Revelation and the Bible

As so many Christian writers and theologians have pointed out, a group's attitude toward the Bible is an important indicator of its orthodoxy or its error. The new religious movements downplay, distort and, in some instances, displace the Bible. The eclectic groups consider the Bible to be one book among many sacred writings from various religions—all of which can be beneficial and capable of generating spiritual awareness. Such groups usually teach that there are many paths to salvation and that all are equally valid. Jesus said, "I am the way and the truth and the life. No one comes to the Father except through me" (Jn 14:6).

The Unification Church clearly states its view of Scripture: "It may be displeasing to religious believers, especially to Christians, to learn that a new expression of truth must appear. They believe that the Bible, which they now have, is perfect and absolute in itself. . . . The Bible, however, is not the truth itself, but a textbook teaching the truth."[3]

This new truth is said to clarify and expand upon the Bible The

Unification Church teaches that God has progressively revealed truth to humankind, and whereas the Bible was adequate for people living during the times of the Old and New Testaments, it no longer fully meets the sophisticated needs of contemporary man. "Intellectual people cannot be satisfied by merely hearing that Jesus is God's Son and the Savior of mankind."[4] According to Moon, Jesus died on the cross before he could successfully complete his mission and without being able to say all that he wanted to say. In a distorted interpretation of John 16:13, Moonies teach that the "words Jesus left unuttered" are being revealed today through the Holy Spirit in the form of a "new truth" which will "elucidate the fundamental contents of the Bible so clearly that everyone can recognize and agree with it."[5]

The Unification Church, like many of the new religious movements, believes in the necessity of extrabiblical revelation. For the Moonies, the *Divine Principle* takes precedence over the Bible. This is made clear in Frederick Sontag's controversial book on Moon and his church. "All doctrine and practices stem from these teachings. . . . These are new 'scriptures,' like the *Book of Mormon* and Mary Baker Eddy's *Science and Health*. More than the person of Moon, they form the core of the movement spiritually."[6]

The Unification Church also believes in the principle of continuing revelation. The introductory section of the *Divine Principle* concludes with this admission: "The Divine Principle revealed in this book is only part of the new truth. . . . We believe with happy expectation that as time goes on, deeper parts of the truth will be continually revealed."[7]

Moonies view Scripture not as truth itself but as a lamp which illuminates the truth. "Its mission is to shed the light of truth. When a brighter light appears, the mission of the old one fades."[8] Following this view, the new light of Moon shines brighter than the older light, Jesus Christ. In contrast, biblical Christians believe that God's Word is changeless and is totally adequate for the needs of humankind, yesterday, today and forever.

Apostle Stevens (now deceased), of the aberrant Christian group known as the Walk, also spoke of "a progressive unfolding of the Scriptures" in a manual of doctrinal teachings entitled *The First Principles*. Stevens stated that each generation of Christians will enter into newly restored Bible experiences and patterns. "It will continue to be so—tomorrow's light will be brighter than today's."[9]

Stevens and his apostolic company stress the importance of "real revelation teaching" and the "new levels of revelation" which they believe God is leading them into. "While a bow is made in the direction of acknowledging the inspiration and authority of scriptures, it is clear that in practice the source of teaching is not primarily the Bible but contemporary revelation."[10] Of his own ministry, Stevens boasted:

The Lord has led me by revelation in every service. . . . I do not try to preach difficult, deep sermons, and yet there is a depth to them that reaches to everyone because I look to the Lord for revelation. I have been preaching almost wholly by revelation for many months. Sometimes the Lord will keep me up all night talking about something. When I speak it, it is a fantastic flow that moves the people tremendously because it is alive, it is real revelation.[11]

The need for Christians to have "direct revelation from the Lord" is a pervasive theme in Stevens's published sermons and other writings. "We cannot underestimate the value of revelation. . . . You must be open to a flow of revelation from the Lord."[12] "God has given the apostolic ministry a unique ability to break into new levels in God and then impart them to the people. . . . This Walk is ordained to come into tremendous wisdom and revelation about the age to come."[13] Stevens talked about "opening up a new line of truth and a new level of revelation" as part of "revelation worship—a worship in which God reveals to us directly, so that the intermediary channels of ministry will not be necessary."[14]

Demonstrating the typical "they and us" mentality of most cult leaders, Apostle Stevens warned his followers that they would be "maligned and slandered" by opponents because of their unusual teachings. "By present standards this Walk is most unorthodox," admitted Stevens in one of his frequent denunciations of established churches.[15] Beware of the kind of orthodoxy, warned Stevens, that in the name of defending the truth builds "walls against God's revelation."[16]

Sun Myung Moon also recognizes that traditional Christian churches are not going to rise up and call him blessed. "From the Christian church's point of view, my teaching, the new revelation, is not only extraordinary but revolutionary. I can understand why Christians call us heretics."[17] This is of no concern to Moon, however, because he is convinced that God does not consider him to be heretical. "From God's point of view, my revelation is deeply orthodox."[18]

Lord of the Second Advent

One of the major reasons Moon is considered heretical by orthodox Christianity is that he teaches that Jesus failed to achieve *full* salvation for humanity; he failed to bring about physical as well as spiritual salvation. Therefore, according to Moon, another messiah—the Lord of the Second Advent—must come to earth during the present "Completed Testament Age" in order to fulfill Christ's mission. Many, if not most, of Moon's followers believe that he is this expected messiah come in the flesh. Moon himself has been careful not to publicly confirm (or deny) such an assertion. He has, however, alluded to that possibility in a published interview with Professor Sontag: "I must serve as God's instrument to bring about the salvation of the world."[19]

Although very cautious in their public statements regarding Moon's alleged messiahship, leaders of the Unification Church have from time to time revealed their true feelings in talks to the membership. Neil Salonen, former president of the Unification Church in America, said in 1975: "We can be connected with the

Messiah. We have to feel that Father [Moon] came and suffered, not just for all mankind, but for us—and because of his suffering, we can be saved. Therefore, he is our personal savior."[20] Elsewhere Salonen affirms the messiahlike qualities of "Father" Moon:

When we study Father's testimony, we have to realize that Father suffered and struggled so much not merely to accomplish his own mission. He had to suffer for our sakes, for our sins, to redeem our fallen nature. . . . In the end, we have to think just as the most fundamental Christians have thought about Jesus: Father suffered and was tortured not just for his universal mission and not just for our redemption but for *my* redemption.[21]

The average Moonies which the public encounters on the street corner are often reluctant to categorically state that Moon is the messiah. Their responses are usually ambiguous. Not infrequently, they have denied that the Unification Church teaches that Moon is indeed the Lord of the Second Advent. In-house publications directed at "members only" are far more candid, however, in that they seem to take Moon's exalted status for granted. For example, in 1972 the faithful were castigated because during a speaking tour of America Moon's audiences weren't up to expectations. "In one city after another the halls weren't filled. Empty seats in front of the Lord of the Second Advent, and it was our responsibility!"[22] In another limited circulation newsletter, Miss Kim, a long time member and leader of the Moon movement, is quoted as saying, "He is the Messiah not because he is perfect, but because he overcame Satan."[23]

This imperfect messiah is variously referred to as "Master," "Father," the "True Man," "Our Leader," the "Wayshower" and "the Channel through whom the blessing is brought." The messianic mission of Moon is in a state of constant precariousness. Its success is entirely dependent on the loyalty of his followers. As Sontag points out:

Moon cannot fulfill the messiah's role by himself. Jesus was not able to carry his mission to full fruition, not through his own fault but as a result of the failure of those around him. The realization of that fact accounts for the intensity of discipleship in Moon's movement, but it also implies that Moon could fail in his leadership. Nothing is guaranteed to him except the call to the attempt at this time.[24]

This is a telling commentary on this "maybe" messiah who commands the obedience and loyalty of hundreds of thousands of followers around the world! Nothing is guaranteed! The Wayshower may lose his way! If his mission turns out to be a failure, he can always blame his followers. Perhaps this explains why Moon once told his flock: "I am a slavedriver to drive you out on a world mission."

In his nine-hour interview with Professor Sontag (supposedly the last he will grant—cver), Moon commented on his mission and revealed another aspect of the systematized error which characterizes his teaching:

Until God's goal is reached, no one can really rest or relax. Just becoming a Christian is not our goal. My goal is the salvation of the world, and that's not even the end of it. . . . We are going to liberate God. We are going to liberate Jesus Christ. We are going to liberate them from sorrow, from brokenheartedness.

I have consummated my personal mission here on earth. Therefore, whether I remain here on earth or whether I am taken to the spirit world doesn't make any difference. Our movement has laid a firm foundation. . . . It will go on without me and the kingdom of God shall become a reality here on earth.[25]

Angels of Light

As we noted earlier, Jim Jones proclaimed himself to be God. He saw himself as a reincarnation of Jesus. He denounced the Bible as a pack of lies but continued to quote it where it suited and supported him. Satan often comes in the guise of a very religious being, as an angel of light. Evil often lurks behind a benign persona. False religion is both alluring and deceiving because it comes packaged with so many half-truths. And for many persons embarked on a genuine religious search, it is not always easy to distinguish the truly spiritual from the sham, the counterfeit.

False religion is characteristically a religion of concealment and secrecy. Whether it is the "deeper truths" of aberrant Christian movements or the "hidden teachings" of Eastern mysticism, esotericism is at the core of all cultic belief. There is a "deliberately created gap between the truth about the cult which is given to the 'inner circle' and a misleading image which is projected to the public at large."[26] Members of the Church Universal and Triumphant, for example, who participate in the Keepers of the Flame Fraternity, are required to sign the following pledge:

Bearing in mind that the Keepers of the Flame Lessons are outer signs of the inner initiations of my soul and the sealing of my consciousness in the law vouchsafed to me in the retreats of the Brotherhood, I shall keep the trust that is placed in me by keeping the lessons confidential, sharing them with no one. And I shall see to it that the lessons are either burned or returned to you upon my transition [death] from this plane.

Scripture states that false teachers are secret and destructive. "But there were also false prophets among the people, just as there will be false teachers among you. They will secretly introduce destructive heresies, even denying the sovereign Lord who bought them—bringing swift destruction on themselves. Many will follow their shameful ways and will bring the way of truth into disrepute" (2 Pet 2:1-2).

There is no room for secrecy or "special discoveries" in biblical Christianity. With regard to the God of the Bible, the Christian can unequivocally assert that he has revealed, not concealed. Speaking of the central facts concerning Christ's life, death and resurrection, Paul writes, "This was not done in a corner" (Acts 26:26).

The task of every true minister of the gospel is to take the mysteries of God and make them plain. The secret is out! Jesus Christ is Lord!

EIGHT

Psychic, Occult and Sexual Dimensions

One of the hallmarks of false religion is the corruption and distortion of human sexuality. Most of the new religious cults depart from biblical principles with regard to the roles of sex and marriage. There is usually a preoccupation with sexuality— either in the direction of promiscuity and unconventional behavior or in the form of a denial or repression of sexual urges.

The leadership of Faith Tabernacle teaches that sex is evil and should be engaged in only for purposes of procreation (although having children is also strongly discouraged). A former member states that the leader, Mrs. Daries, would exert pressure on married couples to sleep in separate bedrooms to help insure a life of holiness. Sex was never to take place after church services (which were held almost nightly) because it took one's thoughts off God. Wives were instructed to dress and undress in the closet. Marriages were both arranged and broken up by the leadership. Members were forced to write letters of confession in which sex was discussed in detail.

In his excellent book on the Unification Church, Jerry Yamamoto makes note of "the presence of sexuality in every facet of Moon's life and thought."[1] Sexual irregularities involving leadership persons have been alleged by ex-members of the Community Chapel, the Walk, the Children of God and, most notably, the People's Temple. In an interview with the *Los Angeles Times,* a Jonestown survivor stated: "Jim Jones was a homosexual. To make himself feel comfortable, he made all the other men say they were homosexuals, too. One older fellow got up at a meeting and said, 'I never had feelings for another man. I've been married for twenty years.' Right away, three other brothers got up and said this first man had asked them for sex. Jones had set it up, you see."[2]

Mel White reports that Jones was threatened by the notion of intimacy inside the group with anyone but himself. "He used his sexual powers both to keep people loyal to himself and to keep people from building relationships with one another that might lead to his eventual undoing."[3] He used sex to control, intimidate and blackmail. "Husbands and wives were forced to sleep with different partners. Jones had a special habit of arranging for a husband or wife to walk into the room as he was seducing the person's spouse. Jones required confessions on a regular basis, statements describing sexual perversions or acts of violence that had supposedly been committed."[4]

Sex and the Children of God

Of all the new religious movements, the Children of God (now called the Family of Love) are most notorious for their preoccupation with sexual matters. Founder-leader David ("Moses") Berg distributes his teachings to his followers and the public in the form of "Mo Letters" which frequently contain sexually oriented artwork and titles like "Sex Works!" "In the Beginning—Sex!" and "Revolutionary Love Making." He has urged his female followers to engage in a modern version of the ancient practice of religious prostitution. "There is nothing wrong with a sexy conversion. We believe sex is a human necessity, and in certain cases we may go to bed with someone to show people God's love."[5]

According to an interview with ex-Children of God members published in *Christianity Today*, extramarital sex and wife-swapping are commonplace in the cult. "Married couples were encouraged as a group to participate in 'skinny-dipping'—swimming in the nude. It was considered unrevolutionary not to participate. . . . It was also policy for all married couples to attend evening 'leadership training' sessions. . . . These sessions would be held by David Berg, and no matter what subject they started out about they always ended up on the subject of sex, with David Berg quite frequently leading the couples into a mass lovemaking session while he looked on."[6]

A few years ago "Father David" began to teach that the injunction found in Acts 2:44 concerning having "everything in common" applied even to husbands and wives. A leaflet produced in April 1978 by the group illustrates their position: "Love not only in word but in deed and in truth—share your money, clothing, housing, education and even sex with those that have need." Berg issued what has become known as the "flirty fish policy," which instructed female members to be "hookers for Jesus." They were admonished to keep reports of their sexual encounters with "fish" (outsiders) as well as report the number of decisions for Christ made as a result of sexual witness. COG women were told to ply their fish with wine, consuming it "prayerfully . . . and in sober moderation." The Mo Letter which begins by asking, "Are you willing to be bait?" ends with the prayer, "May God help us all to be flirty little fishes for Jesus to save lost souls!"

Perhaps the ultimate indicator of Mo Berg's descent into pornography and blasphemy is his statement regarding Jesus: "From

87

personal revelations and Bible study, I am convinced that Jesus Himself could have enjoyed His Father's own creation of sexual activity with some of the women He lived with, particularly Mary and Martha, and yet without sin. Why should it have been a sin for Christ to have enjoyed sex that He Himself had created?"[7]

While sexual self-aggrandizement is often the norm in the Children of God, sexual abstinence and regulation are characteristic of the Hare Krishna movement. "The rules of celibacy are broken for couples desiring to have children. They may have sexual relations once a month on the most auspicious day for conception. Because sex like everything is performed for Krsna's pleasure, the couple must chant fifty rounds on their japa beads for purification before engaging in sexual activity."[8]

As is the case in a number of the new religious movements, women members of Hare Krishna are relegated to a low status vis-a-vis males:

ISKCON women are discouraged from doing anything on their own, so they cannot even walk out of the temple without permission. If they go out to do errands, they are always accompanied by another ISKCON member. A woman who is married should ask her husband's permission to do anything beyond her prescribed temple duties. Ideally, the woman must be completely submissive and a constant servant to her husband.[9]

Peter Marin writes about Naropa Institute, a Buddhist school in Boulder, Colorado, founded by a Tibetan monk known as Trungpa. Each summer hundreds of students come to this retreat in the Rockies to imbibe Eastern wisdom and learn meditative techniques. In addition to being introduced to Buddhist ideas, students engage in considerable merrymaking, drinking and sex. At one party where the spiritual master himself was drunk, "A woman is stripped naked, apparently at Trungpa's joking command, and hoisted into the air by the Vajra guards, and passed around."[10]

Bhagwan Shree Rajneesh advocated sexual experimentation and frequently began his discourses with an off-color joke. Ex-members report that public nudity and sexual activity were not uncommon in the group, a fact that is supported by the documentary film, *Ashram.*

From Sex to the Occult

The close association of sexuality and spirituality in cultic religion often leads to involvement in psychic and occult practices. The word *occult* means hidden from view, beyond the range of ordinary knowledge. The aura of mystery and the unknown which surrounds cult leaders and their teachings is one of the reasons New Age religion is popular. People are impressed and intrigued by the mysterious, the powerful.

One of the goals of all religion, including Christianity, is the achieving of spiritual power. By its very nature, all spiritual power is ambiguous. For the Christian, the crucial determinant is: *What is the source of the spiritual power in question?* Christians must be aware of the presence of a real spiritual power which underlies the teachings and practices of the cults. Not only is it real power, but it works! Hindu miracle workers can and do perform amazing feats. Self-improvement organizations like Scientology and the Forum are successful because their clients claim they are helped. A woman who took the Forum training describes a healing she experienced: "When the trainer focused on all that, it was indescribable. It was too much; the pain in my legs was so intense. Then I felt waves of heat come over me, and all the pain went away. . . . Since that day I haven't had a single pain in my legs."[11]

Ex-Moonies report having had very real—sometimes frightening, sometimes ecstatic—spiritual experiences: "I prayed even harder and just then I felt like everything I was saying was being sucked into a vacuum. When I stood up I felt like thin air; I had to brace myself. I felt this energy, it was kind of an ecstasy. It just flowed through me like a sensation of tingling. It sent shocks through me, and I equated it with divine love."[12] Another former member of the Unification Church relates a similar experience: "I felt a tingling in my back like raindrops, and I thought *Wow, wow, this is a sign!* It felt cool; it lasted about ten seconds, like God was about twenty feet above me with a little sprinkler."[13]

TM works; yoga works; Satan works! As Christians, we must be careful to discern true spiritual power from Satan's counterfeit. With worldwide interest in the occult and spiritism on the increase, Paul's warning is particularly relevant at this time: "For our struggle is not against flesh and blood, but against the rulers, against the authorities, against the powers of this dark world and against the spiritual forces of evil in the heavenly realms" (Eph 6:12).

The dark world of psychic and occult phenomena is in evidence throughout the new religious movements. David Berg claims to have received messages from "spiritual counselors" (what the Bible calls "familiar spirits"). His primary occult spirit guide is named Abrahim, a supposed gypsy king who has been dead for a thousand years. He also claims to have had spirit contact with Rasputin, Joan of Arc and Merlin the magician. Berg has visited fortune tellers and astrologers and had sexual relations with spirit beings whom he calls "goddesses."[14]

Sun Myung Moon claims to be in constant communication with the spirit world. In a speech delivered in April 1965, Moon announced, "We must obtain the truth and the power from the spirit world. . . . Many of my followers, after some years of guidance by the spirit world, have been suddenly led to me."

Elsewhere, Moon has stated to his followers that he has "subjugated Satan on the spirit side. I have talked with many, many masters, including Jesus. . . . They have subjected themselves to me in terms of wisdom. After I won the victory, they surrendered. If you study the Principle . . . if you firmly stand on the Principle, I will appear to you in spirit and teach you everything that you need to know." A long-time follower of Moon has stated: "To us, he sometimes materializes, sometimes he just appears to us in spirit or we hear his voice from a great distance."

Another older member of the Unification Church makes this

revealing comment: "In the early days of our group, he would read our minds. . . . Many such things happened. It was awesome. But he had to work that way, because in that stage he had to encourage people to believe in him."[15]

A British member of Moon's church is quoted as saying that "the spirit of George Fox, the founder of Quakerism, bowed low before her, saying that while they were sitting in chairs, he and those [spirits] with him were bowing with their faces to the floor, because they were so unworthy to be there with Master [Moon]. He said that while on earth he hated the sound of church bells on Sunday morning, but he wishes that all the bells of London would ring for Master."[16]

One of the most controversial aspects of the Church of the Living Word (The Walk) is its involvement in psychic and borderline occult practices. The leaders, most of whom have conventional evangelical backgrounds, deny any mystical or psychic dimensions in their worship and church life. Objective outside observers and ex-members disagree. The group's own literature presents incriminating evidence. Apostle Stevens himself has stated, "Open your spirit to Him and to each other, and soon you will understand that the Bible is more of a mystical book than people ever dared dream. . . . We may be criticized for some of the things we do, but there is nothing fanatical about it. . . . Newcomers often look at what we do . . . as though it is too mystical and far out; but yet they see that things work. The realm of the spirit is an unseen realm and you can't put it in a test tube or weigh it. Yet it is very real."[17]

Stevens reminds his followers, "In your present state, even though you are a Christian, your eyes are still not seeing the spirit world; your ears are not hearing the spirit world. . . . You must work your way up to the higher plane."[18] "If you move on higher in the spirit world . . . the demon world will fade out."[19]

The Walk places considerable emphasis on the "laying on of hands." One manual describes the procedure for joining hands in a circle (forming a "glory chain") in order to transfer the "force of God's blessing": "With palms up, place your right hand under your neighbor's left hand. The blessing you are sending flows out from the palm of your right hand, and he receives it through the back of his left hand."[20] The same manual tells what to do when the person is not receiving much in the way of blessing:

Sometimes the vibrations of your spirit are too low and not much blessing comes through. When you raise your vibrations to the level where the blessing is flowing, you can tune in to it. It is like dialing a radio. When you want a certain station you dial that level on your condenser and the music comes through loud and clear. How do you raise your vibrations? Without any actual movement, get the feeling of liking inside your head, above the ears. In the process of doing that, you do something within your mind to lift you to a higher vibration.[21]

Stevens taught that a form of astral projection may be practiced by Christians. By means of projecting the human spirit "you could, by your spirit being quite free, go to another person and participate in what he is doing, and help him with ministry beyond physical limitations."[22] Stevens cited scriptural support for this practice (1 Cor 5:3-4) by concluding that Paul was able to project his spirit to Corinth from a distant point.

The Walk attaches great spiritual significance to physical "body signs." In a booklet designed to help pastors "interpret" such signs, Stevens wrote:

A sharp stabbing pain under the fifth rib may be a sign of treachery underfoot. . . . An itching sensation in the ear generally indicates confusion or deception, or the fact that the enemy is working at you. . . . If Satan is trying to get through, you will feel a pinching sensation on your shoulders, sometimes very hard. . . . Since the rectal area deals with the elimination process of the body, a sign there would indicate the elimination of spiritual poisons . . . . Signs come in the reproductive organs . . . as an evidence that God is starting a creative work in your life. . . . A great deal can be revealed through the thumb. . . . If someone is set against me I get a certain sign in my thumb . . . he is antagonistic toward the apostolic ministry. Usually I get a pain in my heart simultaneously with the sign in the thumb.[23] Christians need to pay heed to the words of Paul, who warned that false apostles would do "mighty works" and would deceive many. "For such men are false apostles, deceitful workmen, masquerading as apostles of Christ. And no wonder, for Satan himself masquerades as an angel of light" (2 Cor 11:13-14).

Staff members of the Spiritual Counterfeits Project have concluded that the element of the demonic is perhaps *the* crucial explanatory factor in understanding cultic behavior today:

Our research into cults both large and small has revealed that the lowest common denominator is often that of direct spirit influence. Jones claimed to be the oracle or medium for discarnate entities from another galaxy. He also said he was the reincarnation of Jesus, Buddha, and Lenin. The lying spirits that seemingly possessed him gave him great powers of charisma and control. The virtually hypnotic and psychic hold that Jim Jones had on his followers is common among many major cults whose leaders claim contact with "familiar spirits," gods, and demons. In fact, it seems to be a prerequisite for illicit, occult spiritual power.[24]

In his important book *Unmasking the New Age*, Douglas Groothuis describes the subtle, mystical appeal of New Age thinking. Because overt occultism is not attractive to many moderns, the New Age movement "packages its occult philosophy in culturally attractive and appealing wrappings. It enlists the respectability of science, psychology, medicine and established culture in general to further its appeal."[25]

NINE

What Is a Family to Do?

Cults capitalize on the human need for association, for belonging, for family. Many of the new religious movements which are communal in style actually become surrogate families for their members. Leaders are sometimes referred to as "spiritual parents" or "parents in the Lord." So strong is the influence of the cult that a member's natural parents are usually relegated to an inferior status, sometimes totally rejected.

In a publication of the Body of Christ, a small aberrant Christian group in southern California, members are told: "Be prepared to switch your loyalty from your natural family to God's family. . . . All that we have known and experienced as a natural family has to die. Those blood ties are filthy rags unto God."[1] The group goes so far as to proscribe any affection for pets. In a tape-recorded talk to her followers, founder Marie Kolasinski states: "All of our natural affection [must go]. That means our affections towards our families, our affections towards our dog, our affections towards our wives, our husbands, our children."

The severing of all ties with one's family is an integral part of the process of psychological kidnaping which new members often undergo. If parents and other family members can be recast into the role of agents of Satan or viewed as representatives of the corrupt old order, the young recruit is even more effectively bonded to the cult. At best, parents are tolerated and pitied; at worst, scorned and abandoned.

An ex-member of Faith Tabernacle tells how the leadership of that cult used Scripture to reinforce their view that all contacts with parents and close relatives must be cut off. "We were taught that even Jesus said that your worst enemies are those of your own household. Your parents are back in the kindergarten stage of church. They may be Christians, but they are hindering you from going on with God." Members were told that the "cutting off" process could include insults and hate letters directed at parents. "In so doing we were told that all our bridges would be completely burned and family members would never accept us back if we ever did decide to leave." Another example of a not-so-subtle control mechanism.

Children are sometimes raised communally with their age peers in organizations like Synanon and the Hare Krishna movement. In several new religious groups where families are present there have been reports of child abuse and neglect. A former member of Faith Tabernacle reports that a particularly pretty little girl—just learning to talk—was forced to repeat "I ugly, I ugly" over and over so that she would not develop pride. In the same cult teen-age children were forced to slap their parents who were being disciplined by the group.

Mothers who are members of the River of Life Ministry are told that undue attachment to children can be spiritually harmful. One former member reports that she was physically restrained from comforting and consoling her son after he had been injured in a fall. She was told that she had a "spirit of motherhood," which was an evil spirit in the eyes of this group. Marie Kolasinski of the Body of Christ movement warns: "God is going to take away every idol from the land. If your children are your idol, He's going to take them from you."

Numerous instances of marriages being broken up by cult leaders have been reported to me. The adversarial impact of cult membership on marriage and the family is illustrated by this incredible statement by David Berg, prophet of the Family of Love:

God breaks up marriages in order that he might join each of the parties together to himself. He rips off wives, husbands or children to make up his bride if the rest of the family refuses to follow. He is the worst "ripper-offer" of all. God is the greatest destroyer of home and family of anybody! . . . If you have not forsaken your husband or wife for the Lord at some time or another, you have not forsaken all.[2]

This diabolical undercutting of the God-ordained institution of the family is one of the most tragic by-products of the emergence of extremist cults. In addition to the parents and other family members themselves, perhaps only those of us who have counseled or have had sustained contact with parents of cult members can comprehend the magnitude of the problem. The heartache, the anxiety, the feelings of hopelessness and frustration which these parents feel must surely be one of the major tragedies of our day. The plight of parents was dramatized by the events in Jonestown, although many thousands of parents continue to face uncertainty and uneasiness over the ultimate fate of their children enmeshed in current cultic movements, some of which have received little attention in the media.

Not all parents are worried about their offspring's involvement in new religious movements. Some see the dramatic personality changes which have occurred in their sons and daughters as an improvement over past association in the drug scene or counter-culture. Other young people caught up in the cults have no real family to relate to outside the group. Even if they wanted to leave the cultic life, they have few, if any, resources or caring contacts "on the outside" to assist them in the resocialization process. After years of developing strong dependency ties to the cult, it is diffi-cult—and often frightening—for an individual to actually follow through on a decision to leave.

What alternatives exist for concerned parents who have a son or daughter in an extremist cult? They can patiently wait it out, hop-ing that someday something will occur in the group itself or in the mind of the member which will trigger a voluntary exit. For parents who occasionally see their child and maintain some degree of con-tact, this can be a very painful period. The months and years go by, and with them educational and career opportunities which prob-ably never will be recouped. Parents see the best, most productive years of a young person's life essentially wasted in a cult. Even more trying is the experience of parents who see the mental and physical health of their children impaired and are powerless to do anything about it. All too frequently parents echo the lamentation of Jere-miah· "Those I cared for and reared, my enemy has destroyed" (Lam 2:22).

A much more precarious and controversial option for parents of a cult member is to go the route of deprogramming. This word became a part of the American vocabulary a few years ago when Ted Patrick began snatching cult members away from their groups. Patrick put each cultist through intense, emotional sessions de-signed to force them to think on their own and then, it was hoped, decide to leave the cults.

Parents who see no other way to retrieve a son or daughter from an extremist group have elected to hire deprogrammers and essen-tially kidnap their own children. Parents hope that this forced sep-aration from the cult combined with the input of the deprogram-ming team (which usually includes young people who have been members of the group in question) will have the desired impact. The process can take a few hours or a few days, and it can be very expensive for the parents, who must pay the fees charged by the deprogrammers, their transportation and expenses, as well as the motel bills for the actual site of the deprogramming.

The morality of involuntary deprogramming and the techniques involved in the process have been the subjects of much heated debate in the media and elsewhere. "Its definition and connotation are largely dependent on who and what you read and who and what you choose to believe. There are conflicting reports with regard to the purposes, procedures and personnel involved in deprogramming. . . . Depending on one's perspective, deprogrammers are viewed as either 'latter day vigilantes' or courageous rescuers of ensnared youth."[3]

Because they have lost members as a result of deprogramming, the cults have been very vocal in their denunciation of the practice, calling it a violation of the principle of religious liberty through forced confinement and the use of "mental torture." Victor Paul Wierwille, former leader of The Way, viewed deprogramming as a "scheme invented by the Devil, fostered by some denominational churches troubled by unsound doctrine and dwindling congregations, and supported by unwary parents distressed by the neuroses of our times."[4] Cults tend to define all attempts to dissuade an individual from cult membership—whether that attempt is in a voluntary or involuntary context—as deprogramming.

Many ex-cult members view their deprogramming favorably; others have major reservations about the tactics and techniques employed, while not questioning the motives or sincerity of the deprogrammer. Still others return to the cults. For them the process was unsuccessful, and the alienation from parents is greater than before. A flurry of lawsuits involving both parents and deprogrammers has not resolved the controversy completely, although the level of deprogramming activity has dropped sharply in recent years because of the legal difficulties.

There are some deprogrammers still active in the United States, despite costly legal battles and mixed reaction in the press. Others now prefer to be called "exit counselors" rather than deprogrammers and work with clients who agree to voluntary and noncoercive counseling. Few if any professionals are directly involved in deprogramming activities. Some deprogrammers operate in association with rehabilitation programs—usually small and constantly facing legal and financial trouble. Most deprogrammers, if involved in rehabilitation work at all, focus on the physical, social and psychological needs of ex-members; hardly any attempt is made to meet the spiritual needs of people. A few evangelical Christians identify themselves as exit counselors and attempt to fill the spiritual vacuum remaining after someone leaves a cult, with a positive witness to the redeeming work of Jesus Christ.

Critics charge that deprogramming and exit counseling are subject to abuse. The question has been raised about who decides which groups are indeed "cults" and whether such procedures might be used by parents wishing to extract a child from a marginal or even mainstream religious group. There are non-Christian parents, for example, who consider Jews for Jesus and Campus Crusade for Christ to be cultic. Where is the line drawn? On the other hand, supporters of deprogramming argue that abuse is rare because parents and society can distinguish between truly destructive cults and "legitimate" religious organizations. Opponents maintain that coercive methods used to change a person's faith are a violation of freedom of religion. They assert that true "brainwashing" is rare and difficult to prove.

Many ex-cult members are grateful that their parents intervened and had them deprogrammed. "These people say that they had felt themselves powerless to carry out their desire to leave because of psychological and social pressures from companions and officials inside. They often speak of a combination of guilt over defecting and fear of the cult's retaliation—excommunication—if they tried."[5]

Christian parents must approach with caution any procedure which might involve the use of force and illegal acts. However, to parents who have tried everything short of force, including prayer, and who have seen no results and have little prospect of regaining a son or daughter, that advice is of small comfort. It is my opinion, nevertheless, that patience and prayer combined with a hopeful and sustained love—despite the desperately trying circumstances—is an appropriate Christian response.

Parents who decide against some type of deprogramming must make every attempt to keep channels of communication open with their children. While they need not disguise their honest feelings about cult leaders and cult practices, parents should seek to keep to a minimum those discussions which lead to confrontation and further alienation. Wisdom and discernment as well as the strength and help of the Holy Spirit are continuing prerequisites for Christian parents with children in such groups. Parents must be fully informed about cults and may wish to counsel with a pastor or some other Christian professional who is knowledgeable in this area. They will also want to avail themselves of the resources provided by the various organizations—such as the American Family Foundation (Weston, Mass.)—which are active in most sections of the United States.

Preventative Actions

What can parents do to prevent and ward off the possibility of their children's involvement in cults and aberrant Christian movements? Because of the seductive and Satanic nature of false religion, there is probably no infallible insurance available, even after young people have been alerted. Christian parents who have conscientiously done their best, with God's help, in rearing children who then join cults often suffer tremendous guilt. They constantly ask, "Where did we go wrong?" As we have seen, the reasons young people join new religious groups are varied and complex. In particular cases parents undoubtedly have played a role in the situation. In other instances, young people from what appear to be model families become involved in cults. As professors Stark and Bainbridge point out, "Under present sociocultural conditions, cults can have great success recruiting persons who are fully normal in terms of almost any characteristic one wants to measure."[6]

Still, one of the best protections against the possibility of cultic involvement is a strong, supportive, loving family in which communication is open and honest and in which children develop early a positive self-image and a healthy sense of autonomy. A secure young person who thinks for himself or herself and yet values and accepts advice from adults is less likely to feel the need to search out a rigidly authoritarian group for direction. Parents who listen to and relate to a young person as an adult-in-the-making will win the confidence of their children.

Christian parents who wish to prevent the loss of a son or daughter to cultic religion must be prepared to work hard at cultivating meaningful, loving and flexible relationships within the family unit. Young adults need affirmation and acceptance, not merely toleration or routine attention. They need positive Christian role models—people who can be authoritative without being authoritarian.

Most important, parents need to encourage their children to have a firm faith in Christ as personal Savior and a biblical understanding of that faith. People—whether young or old—who seek after "new truth" frequently have little of the "old truth." Those who have firmly established their own values and goals in the framework of their own Christian faith are not likely to find cultic alternatives appealing. Even secular observers recognize that fact. "Persons truly dedicated to one religion are not ready converts to another. . . . Church membership and membership in a conservative denomination are preventives against cultism. The unchurched and those affiliated with the more secularized denomination are more open to cult involvement."[7]

TEN

The Response of the Church

T he newer cultic movements, especially the derivatives of evangelical Christianity, are uniformly antagonistic toward and critical of traditional, established churches and denominations. John Robert Stevens of the Walk has stated that "a denominational people is always a spiritually immature people. . . . It is a fact of history that there is not one denomination or organization that has opened the doors to further revelation and light from the scriptures after it organized."[1] Members of the Walk refer to conventional Christian churches as "the old order."

Hobart Freeman of Faith Assembly would tell his followers, "God deliver us from denominational bondage." Community Chapel's Donald Barnett speaks disdainfully of "the church world." The Family of Love (formerly Children of God) refer to church members as "systemites." The *Divine Principle* of the Unification Church describes Christians as "blindly keeping the conventional attitude of faith."[2] It is no doubt significant that the leaders of most aberrant Christian groups at one time were associated with established denominations. Somewhere along the ecclesiastical trail they were either kicked out of or became disenchanted with institutional religion and decided to launch their own ego-satisfying alternatives.

The Way's Victor Paul Wierwille was a minister in the Evangelical and Reformed Church. Apostle Stevens of the Church of the Living Word was at one time ordained by the Assemblies of God. David Berg of the Children of God pastored evangelical churches, and his parents had ties with the Christian and Missionary Alliance. Dr. Hobart Freeman of Faith Assembly was a professor in an evangelical Christian seminary. Jim Jones was a minister in the Disciples of Christ.

Cultic groups claim that established religious organizations are persecuting them. The Unification Church has tried unsuccessfully to gain admission to the National Council of Churches. The Moonies clearly state that Christians (who are "captives to scriptural words") "will be the first to persecute the Messiah at the time of the Second Advent. . . . They can be expected to persecute him and brand him a heretic."[3]

At the same time, members of the Unification Church continue their efforts at influencing and infiltrating Christian churches. In a 1971 newsletter designed for circulation among members only, the Moonies admitted engaging in what they term "church witnessing." "Many have referred to our witnessing in churches as 'fishing in someone else's pond.' We have been accused, and sometimes rightly so, of separating the fringe members."[4] The same newsletter indicated that the Moonies' work at a Baptist church was "bearing fruit."

In another newsletter of the Unification Church, a report indicates that a group of Moonies attended revival services at an evangelical church and gave their testimonies. Members of the Unification Church apparently impressed the pastor, and they were invited back to conduct an entire worship service. "So, as true children of our beloved Parents and our Heavenly Father . . they gave an exciting synopsis of the Principle, based totally on the Bible. The response was beautiful!"[5] The report contains this revealing comment: "When we properly serve the Christians, Father brings the increase."[6]

During such instances of infiltration, Moonies engage in "heavenly deception" by masking their true identity and attempting to sound and act like Christians as much as possible. Former members have indicated that they were encouraged to become active in church choirs, youth groups and related activities in conventional denominational churches in order to locate potential converts for the Unification Church. Because it is a time-consuming means of obtaining recruits, it apparently is no longer practiced to the degree it once was. In conversations with evangelical Christians, however, Moonies quote the Bible freely and sprinkle their rhetoric with such words as "born again." This is consistent with Moon's advice: "Until our mission with the Christian church is over, we must quote the Bible and use it to explain the *Divine Principle*. After we receive the inheritance of the Christian church, we will be free to teach without the Bible."[7]

Aberrant Christian groups like the Walk, Faith Assembly and Faith Tabernacle recruit many of their followers from the ranks of standard evangelical churches, looking for new believers or those who are dissatisfied with their Christian lives. Potential recruits often see the proselytizing groups as having a dynamism and vitality lacking in their own church experience. Aberrant Christian groups have successfully gained converts on the campuses of some Christian colleges and Bible schools.

Several of the new religious movements—notably the Church of Scientology and the Unification Church—have made direct efforts to contact ministers of conventional churches in order to provide information about their organizations and to improve their image

105

in the eyes of church leaders. Mailings sent to pastors may include summaries of basic teachings, reproductions of endorsements from various agencies and individuals, and other public relations materials designed to encourage acceptance and approval of the new religious groups by the clergy.

A cover letter accompanying one such mailing to California pastors by the Unification Church sought to alert ministers to the "gross violations of religious liberty" which were being perpetrated by the government and deprogrammers against new religious groups. Recipients of the letter were urged to express their concern by writing to government officials and sending a copy of such correspondence to the Unification Church "in order to document the response of the religious community." The "Dear Pastor" letter also stated that the Unificationists "would be most happy to meet personally with you and/or your congregation to discuss the theology and lifestyle of the Unification Church."

In 1985 about 300,000 ministers, priests and rabbis throughout the United States received a gift parcel from the Unification Church containing three videotaped lectures and two booklets explaining the church's teachings. The shipping carton was inscribed, "A Gift for You from Some Folks Who Care." The accompanying form letter declared, "Because some are judging us unfairly, please let us tell you what we believe."

Sun Myung Moon was found guilty of tax irregularities and began serving an eighteen-month prison sentence in 1984. As a result, the Unification Church launched a massive campaign to convince religious leaders that Moon was a victim of government persecution and that everyone's religious freedom was at stake. The Moonies were able to garner the support of many conservative (and a few liberal) church people, including some well-known fundamentalists. In May 1984 at a Washington, D.C., rally sponsored by the "Ad Hoc Committee for Religious Freedom," a nationally known fundamentalist proclaimed, "We believe religious rights have been intruded upon and that what is happening to Reverend

Moon is going to happen to us and it is time now for us to take a dramatic stand. . . . In a vital sense his confinement is our confinement." The speaker then announced his willingness to spend one week with Mr. Moon in prison and suggested that other ministers in the audience volunteer to do the same.

Christianity Today reported that "religious freedom" rallies sponsored by the Unification Church around the nation were "drawing thousands of unsuspecting Christians into emotionally charged meetings that portray Moon as a persecuted man of God. No ties with the Unification Church are mentioned in promotional mailings."[8] Pastors were offered expense-paid trips to Washington, D.C., to participate in a huge "Pageant for Religious Freedom" held on July 25, 1984.

In a sense, the imprisonment of Mr. Moon was a tremendous boost for Unificationists who are trying desperately to achieve acceptance and legitimacy in the religious world. A number of religious bodies and evangelical Christian organizations—including the Christian Legal Society and the National Association of Evangelicals—filed friend-of-the-court briefs on Moon's behalf when he stood trial in 1982. Although the Christian organizations involved were quick to point out that their action was in support of the principle of freedom of religion and that they were "friends of the court, not friends of the cult," many evangelicals were disappointed and confused, viewing the supportive action as both misguided and naive.

When Mr. Moon was released from prison in August 1985, fundamentalist leader Jerry Falwell participated in a press conference in Washington and called on President Reagan to issue a full pardon to Moon. A special issue of the *Unification News* published after Moon's release prominently featured the remarks of Rev. Falwell and carried several photographs of him participating in the news conference. Most cults are skillful at using such opportunities to achieve legitimacy by association.

Christian churches must seek to inform and educate their

members concerning the new cultic groups, but they are ill-advised to do so on terms dictated by the cult organizations themselves. Cultic organizations would like nothing better than to set the agenda for any discussion of their own belief systems by having one of their representatives present. Such exposure to carefully camouflaged spiritual error has led to the deception of whole congregations, including their leadership.

The Unification Church has sponsored a series of dialogues at its Barrytown, New York, seminary with a number of evangelical leaders and scholars. At one such encounter, convener Richard Quebedeaux, a United Church of Christ member and author of several books on evangelicalism, made statements indicating that he was favorably impressed by the Moonies. "I have never seen a place where *agape* has worked out so well. Theologically, doctrinally, I think you're wrong. Emotionally, I think you're right. . . . You may be heretics—I'll let God decide that. But I love you, and I believe the world is a better place because of you."[9]

Cult movements also attempt to enhance their cause and improve their image by enlisting members of the academic community in various roles. For example, Professor H. Newton Malony of Fuller Theological Seminary has been an expert witness for the Church of Scientology in a Los Angeles trial. Interviews with American Baptist theologian Harvey Cox of Harvard have appeared in Hare Krishna publications. Philosophy professor Frederick Sontag of Pomona College holds a prominent editorial position in a new publishing house launched by the Unification Church. Every year scientists and other scholars are invited to participate (expense-paid) in conferences sponsored by the Unification Church in various parts of the world.

Churches or other community organizations which sponsor seminars or classes on cults may experience harassment and protest from the cults themselves if it is believed that the content of the presentations will be critical or "antireligious." The pastoral staff of a large Californian Presbyterian church received telephone threats and other forms of harassment as a result of a proposed series of Sunday evening seminars on cultic religion. Opponents of such church-sponsored discussions have been known to demand equal time for their side of the story—an action which amounts to intimidation and threatens freedom of speech.

Evangelical churches must recognize the challenge of the cults to the body of Christ, corporately and individually. In his book *Traps: A Probe of Those Strange New Cults,* Harris Langford urges that special training programs—for young people and adults—be inaugurated in churches to thoroughly acquaint people with the dangers of the new cults. He suggests that a church leader or concerned layperson be assigned the job of becoming an expert in this specialized area of new cults and be given adequate funding to accumulate books, tapes and other materials for educating the congregation.[10]

Denver's Bear Valley Baptist Church has a unique task force on cults which can serve as a model for both evangelizing members of new religious movements and serving as a resource center for a congregation. Several members of the task force have also been involved in a counseling ministry to ex-cult members.

All concerned Christians should keep informed of developments in cultic religion in order to effectively counter the efforts of God's adversary in our world today. There are a number of reputable evangelical organizations actively involved in researching and analyzing new religious groups from a biblical perspective. One organization which has a particularly effective ministry is the Spiritual Counterfeits Project (P. O. Box 4308, Berkeley, CA 94704). Its objective is to "equip Christians with the knowledge, analysis, and discernment that will enable them to understand the significance of today's spiritual explosion" so that they can "bring the good news of Jesus Christ and extend a hand of rescue to those who are in psychological and spiritual bondage."

Though the church must be concerned and informed about new religious movements, its primary task is not to counter the cults but to proclaim the gospel. Paul's exhortation to Timothy is an appropriate response to the cults: Stand firm in the faith and preach the Word. Paul states that false teachers, imposters and charlatans will go "from bad to worse" (2 Tim 3:13). But, as John Stott observes, Christians need have no fear even if falsehood becomes fashionable: "For there is something patently spurious about heresy, and something self-evidently true about the truth. Error may spread and be popular for a time. But it 'will not get very far.' In the end it is bound to be exposed, and the truth is sure to be vindicated. . . . God has preserved his truth in the church."[11]

The church must not be tempted to proclaim the threat of the cults more than the victory of Jesus Christ. It may even be that Satan's strategy might be to use the issue of cults "to decoy Christians into a false alarmism which distracts them from other vital aspects of the Kingdom of God."[12]

The adversary's work is not confined to the cults. A truly Christian response to the cults will also acknowledge Satan's strategy to weaken and subvert the church by pressing it into the world's mold. "It will do very little good for the Church to confront the cults unless we simultaneously confront our own participation in the conditions which have produced them. The ultimate spiritual counterfeit is . . . a Christianity which is culturally co-opted, socially irrelevant, doctrinally correct and spiritually dead."[13]

Christians must also recognize that cultic manifestations are not restricted to exotic Eastern mystical groups or marginal religious sects which appeal to the disadvantaged and undereducated. The aberrant Christian groups which continue to proliferate in mainstream America have the same potential for extremism as the unfamiliar, seemingly more bizarre cults of Eastern origin. The uncomfortable thesis of Mel White's book on the People's Temple is that the victims of Jim Jones came from traditional Christian backgrounds. He issues a warning that the evangelical church cannot take lightly: "They came to Jones from our churches. He provided a warm and caring community to those in need who felt rejected by the churches of their past. And for those who felt their churches were uninterested in the poor and disadvantaged, he provided a program for social change."[14]

This book has told the story of a previously unknown group, Faith Tabernacle, for the first time. The resemblance to Jones's People's Temple is remarkable in many ways. The questions must be asked: How many more Faith Tabernacles are there tucked away in the small towns and cities of America? Why have so many members of aberrant Christian groups like Faith Tabernacle come from traditional Christian churches? What does this exodus from the church say to evangelicalism? What are we doing to diminish the lure of the cults in our own back yard?

ELEVEN

Implications for Society

T he decade of the sixties and the counterculture which emerged from that era were characterized by protest, disenchantment with the establishment and widespread experimentation with alternatives. Americans, especially young Americans, evidenced an openness to new forms of spirituality and new modes of consciousness—new ways of understanding the world. There emerged a privatism and a new interest in the transformation of self. As Glock describes the current scene, "The alternatives most actively pursued . . . are those rooted in revolutionizing not society but the self."[1]

Today many people are experimenting with forms of religious expression outside the frame of reference of most conventional Christians. Organizations like Scientology, Eckankar and TM represent a whole new way of thinking, believing and of defining reality. Young people within and outside the church are growing up as biblical illiterates, unable to ask the right questions and evaluate the new religious movements. They are unaware that our culture is drifting into a post-Christian era characterized by neopaganism and an increasing interest in Eastern mysticism. As a result, large numbers of people are innocently opening themselves up to spiritism and the occult without recognizing the consequences.

Even secular analysts are aware of the potential long-term implications of our complex and fragmented world for its searching idealists. Commenting on the Unification Church, sociologist Irving Louis Horowitz concludes: "Whatever the fate of the Moon movement—whether it goes into rapid decline or slow eclipse—we have entered a period in human history where fragmentation is so thorough and alienation so deep that movements of this type have a compelling power for vast numbers, to the point where the foundations and premises of Western civilization must themselves be reexamined."[2]

Escapism and the Cults

In the midst of profound social and cultural change, young people have sought simplistic answers to complex questions. The new cults provide "a ready-made doctrine for impatient young people, and all those for whom the pursuit of the complex has become a tiresome and fruitless venture."[3] Eastern mystical religions as well as the spiritual technologies advocated by self-improvement and self-awareness groups seek to bypass rational thought and provide escapist solutions to everyday problems. TM, for example, aims at systematically eliminating consciously directed thought and rejects the mind as a means of discovering the truth.

Not only do the cults short-circuit the cognitive and spiritual quests for truth, but they also offer a regressive solution to many of the personal and interpersonal conflicts with which young adults are struggling. The cult and its all-encompassing web becomes a means of avoiding the necessity of coping with the turmoil, confusion and discomfort often associated with the developmental process. The cult presents the young person with the illusion that "here are people you can count on for the rest of your life," who will take care of you and never abandon you.

The pain and uncertainty of young adulthood are alleviated by entry into cultic groups which provide unconditional acceptance and a sense of intimacy. The point here, however, is that despite the group strength and concomitant benefits provided by such movements, the cultic alternative is really an avoidance of maturation and a detour from dealing with developmental conflicts. This is often brought into sharp focus when the cult member, for whatever reason, leaves the group and must face the realities of the "outside" world.

The Problems of Rehabilitation
It is difficult to predict the long-term implications for the individual and for society of sustained membership of large numbers of people in highly structured new religious movements. The potential for personal and social dislocation seems greatest in the strongly authoritarian groups where dependency needs are significant. As Dr. Margaret Singer points out, we can already see something of the impact of these groups as we note the problems former members experience when they try to re-enter normal society: "By now a number of adherents have left such groups, for a variety of reasons, and as they try to reestablish their lives in the mainstream of society, they are having a number of special—and I believe cult-related—psychological problems that say a good deal about what experience in some of these groups can be like."[4]

Society may have to deal with an entirely new category of persons who have become "institutionally dependent" while in the cults. Like inmates of mental hospitals and prisons, whose existence is determined and controlled by the institution with its familiar supports and routines, members of extremist cults may be unprepared for "life outside" after prolonged participation in a cult environment. The loss to the individual and society will be considerable and may be irrevocable. "It may not be possible to make up, at a later phase in the life cycle, the time not now spent in educational or job advancement, in courting, or in rearing one's children."[5]

Facilities which now exist to assist in the rehabilitation and re-socialization of ex-cult members are inadequate. Halfway houses and other agencies staffed with caring, informed professionals and laypersons are desperately needed. The inability to refer to such agencies is a major frustration to those of us who regularly interact with parents and former cult members seeking help. Our society has made provision for assisting ex-alcoholics, young people with drug-related problems, unwed mothers and a host of other social and personal problems, but it has done little to help the victims of the cults.

A few rehabilitation programs are functioning in connection with deprogrammers, but they are costly, understaffed and plagued by almost constant legal problems associated with their sometimes questionable activities in retrieving young people. The need for solidly financed and soundly administered programs to rehabilitate ex-cult members represents a tremendous opportunity for the Christian community. Christians have historically taken leadership roles in areas of great human need. Why have they neglected this obvious and growing social problem?

The Politics of Cults

In addition to the pressing individual, social and spiritual problems which the new religious movements represent, there are political and economic implications which cannot be overlooked. Although not all the new religious groups have an interest in politics, several of them—notably the Unification Church and the TM movement—have been embroiled in political controversy.

Horowitz describes the Unification Church as "a movement without boundaries, expressing belief systems at once political and theological, outlining premises for political action and religious realignment."[6] He makes note of the irony of this Oriental movement, led by a Korean evangelist who speaks little English, making its biggest impact on the center of contemporary Western civilization, the United States:

> But because the Unification church and the Reverend Moon come forth as both a social movement and a civic movement they are able to translate its theological mysticism into events, or at least participation in those events, and for that reason the Unification Church enters world history as neither rationalistic nor mystic but rather as some strange conglomeration of the two fused by the sensuous events of world politics.[7]

The followers of Moon have repeatedly denied charges that they have participated in political activity, claiming that alleged political activities were in fact religious. Interestingly, a 1971 Moonie publication of limited in-house circulation describing a conference for church leaders clearly states, "We launched into a discussion of political work. . . . Neil Salonen gave a presentation dealing with the need to educate those persons in our country who make the decisions that determine our national foreign policy—legislators and other influential persons on Capitol Hill."[8]

More recently a House subcommittee reported that it had found "substantial evidence" that members of the Unification Church had engaged in political activity. This official government investigation concluded:

> Among the goals of the Moon Organization is the establishment of a worldwide government in which the separation of church and state would be abolished and would be governed by Moon and his followers.

> The Moon Organization used church and tax-exempt components in support of its political and economic activities.

> Although many of the goals and activities of the Moon Organization were legitimate and lawful, there was evidence that it had systematically violated U.S. tax, immigration, banking, currency, and Foreign Agents Registration Act laws, as well as

state and local laws relating to charity fraud, and that these violations were related to the Organization's overall goals of gaining temporal power.[9]

The controversy over possible linkages between the Unification Church and the South Korean government, particularly the Korean CIA, is likely to continue. Whether Moon and his devoted followers represent a serious threat in terms of their alleged lobbying efforts in Washington is doubtful.

Yet as Horowitz reminds us, the Moonies' interlocking of ideology and theology is not something Americans can dismiss lightly: "We have yet to cope with a religion that turns political, although we have had less trouble with political movements that turn religious. We understand fanaticism when it progresses from politics to theology. We have less familiarity with absolutist ideologies that drift into authoritarian politics."[10]

The valued American tradition of separation of church and state has been undermined by some of the new religious movements. The Transcendental Meditation movement has introduced TM into the military, prisons and the public schools disguised as a relaxation technique. At least seventeen research grants involving TM have been funded by the federal government. "In its pursuit of governmental support for TM, Maharishi's WPEC [World Plan Executive Council] has been rewarded by expressions of official approval from several states and from a number of cities. Maharishi has addressed the legislatures of Illinois, Michigan, New Hampshire, and Iowa."[11] The governors of both Vermont and Maryland issued World Plan Week proclamations in November 1973.

On October 19, 1977, U.S. District Judge H. Curtis Meanor issued an opinion holding that the Transcendental Meditation movement is religious in nature. The ruling, later affirmed in a United States court of appeals, stated that the teaching of TM in New Jersey public schools represented a violation of the First Amendment to the U.S. Constitution. According to attorney Michael J. Woodruff, "The court's opinion and the efforts of the plaintiffs . . . should be remembered as an effort to protect our constitutional religious freedoms by preventing religious practice and teaching in a secular disguise from infiltrating government processes."[12]

The Economics of Cults

Many cultic groups financially exploit the American public as well as their own members. Adherents of the Hare Krishna sect have been called a public nuisance by officials and airport workers in Los Angeles and other locations. ISKCON members have been accused of harassment, high-pressure tactics and fraudulent misrepresentation while soliciting donations or selling merchandise. Los Angeles Superior Court Judge Julius M. Title accused Hare Krishna devotees of using "unscrupulous" methods in street sales of books and magazines. He indicated that the methods included "misrepresenting both the purpose of the solicitation and the identification of the sellers as something other than the Hare Krishna movement."[13] The judge also cited evidence showing that sales in the street and at Los Angeles International Airport earned the cult $2 million before expenses during the period 1973-76.

Members of the Unification Church have been known to campaign for funds while confined to a wheelchair. Skeptics have questioned whether the Moonies really needed the wheelchairs and have suggested that they were used to gain sympathy and therefore larger contributions. One Moonie detained by police in Billings, Montana, claimed that he had ruined his knees while fundraising and that he hoped to regain the use of his legs eventually. He explained that his situation was not unusual: "It's because the kids are working so hard for what they believe is right. They have worked beyond the point of pain."[14]

I interviewed a former member of the Unification Church who told me that he was personally congratulated by Moon for breaking a record in fundraising. He had raised $1,600 in cash in one day on the streets of San Francisco by selling flowers and candy. Commenting on the gullibility of Americans, this young man said, "I could have told them I was raising money for Bozo the clown, and people would still give money." Within a six-month period he raised over $63,000.

The Moonies' financial success can be attributed in large part to their mobile fundraising teams (MFTs). "Like any other businessman thirsting after a fast buck, Moon simply allocates his manpower resources where the money return is highest."[15] According to one source, the MFT manpower consists of about eight hundred members in the field at any given time.

They work perhaps 300 days a year and average about $150 a day in sales. Most MFTs, whose members sleep in the vans or out of doors and eat frugally, after paying expenses including product cost, manage to send to New York about sixty per cent of their gross income (and some have exceeded ninety per cent). If these numbers are accurate, the Unification Church's gross from the MFTs is well over 20 million dollars a year. Subtracting a national budget of $12 million, the church may be accumulating a net of as much as $10 million a year.[16]

In a declaration filed in connection with divorce proceedings against Apostle Stevens of the Walk, Martha Stevens (his wife of forty years) stated that Stevens's financial empire could amount to $40 million. An investigation by a California newspaper revealed that Stevens had paid a well-known attorney $10,000 plus $125 an hour in the divorce case. The investigation disclosed far-flung real estate holdings, an extensive art collection and $29,000 in silver bars owned by Stevens. It brought to light a Nevada silver mine fraud that allegedly bilked at least $500,000 from members of the Church of the Living Word. According to Mrs. Stevens, "My husband has total control of the church and its funds, and total access to all church finances. He is, in essence, the church himself."[17]

Like other aberrant Christian groups, officials of the Way International are reluctant to discuss finances and membership statistics. Unofficial estimates of the organization's net worth approach $20

120

million. Wierwille's Way received unwanted publicity when a young paraplegic brought suit against the organization for failing to keep a promise. The young man said he gave Way leaders $210,000, two expensive automobiles and other donations in return for a promise that he would be healed and walking again within a year. He won the case and got his money back.[18]

In contrast to the false prophets who make merchandise of people, Paul declared, "Unlike so many, we do not peddle the word of God for profit. On the contrary, in Christ we speak before God with sincerity, like men sent from God" (2 Cor 2:17).

TWELVE

The Challenge of the Cults

Some observers feel that the surge of new religious movements in recent years is merely another passing fad on the religious scene and therefore not worthy of serious attention or concern. Still others, including many parents, are of the opinion that the cults are a growing menace and deserve official investigation if not regulation by the government. Academicians and other professionals involved with the new wave of cultic religion disagree on such issues as brainwashing, manipulation and the potential for violence in the new groups. "There exists a considerable diversity of opinion among scholars . . . about the nature of the social forces fostering unconventional religious expression as well as about government's responsibility vis-á-vis those forces."[1]

Whatever posture is assumed with regard to the new religious movements, certain challenges and lessons present themselves. First, it is evident that the cults are meeting very real needs and that they effect very real changes in the lives of members. Although the thrust of this and similar books is that the overall impact of cultic experience is negative, it should be remembered that even intense, extremist groups—in spite of their confining and controlling environment—can benefit individual members in certain ways. Donna, the young woman whose experiences with Faith Tabernacle were detailed earlier, reported that "there were many good aspects" associated with her cultic sojourn. In terms of personality she changed from an introvert to an extrovert and was able to resolve a number of other personal problems while a member of the group.

Even Jim Jones knew how to affirm people and help them improve their self-images. Speaking of Maria Katsaris, one of Jones's lovers and devoted staff members to the end, an ex-member of the People's Temple makes these observations: "Jones manipulated her so expertly. He made her feel so wanted, so needed—so accepted just as she was. He did everything he could to play to her insecurities. He made her feel important to the functioning of the church from the very beginning."[2]

Apparently, when Maria first came to the church, she was very shy and withdrawn. While in the sect, she matured, discovered her own potential and learned to handle large sums of money. "Jim took away her fear and taught her self-confidence—he knew how to bring out the best in people."[3]

Cult leaders exploit human weaknesses and seek to manipulate individual life situations to the ultimate benefit of the group. The challenge to our society and our churches is to identify the searching, the hurting, the lonely, the unloved people, and to intervene in their lives—in the name of Christ—before they are seduced by the cults. For those already ensnared, we must commend their spiritual search, understand their need to be affirmed and accepted, and offer a viable alternative through the transforming gospel of Jesus Christ.

Barbara Hargrove, a sociologist who has written about the new religious movements, states that we need to take the idealism of young people more seriously. In a society in which full adult status is deferred until lengthy training and study is successfully completed, many young people come to feel that little they do is taken seriously.

The churches do not help matters when they segregate young people into youth groups that discuss problems of adolescence or engage only in recreational activities. What young people need, in the churches and out of them, is a sense of significance. Movements such as Moon's provide it. Privatized churches may have little significance to grant, but often they do not offer young people that which they could provide—a responsible place in their own structure.[4]

The cults represent a challenge to the Christian church because they attract young people who are looking for alternatives to our technological and materialistic way of life. While the church all too frequently has been conformed to the culture and ineffectual in its prophetic role, the proponents of the "new consciousness" have boldly challenged the assumptions of secular society. "They have not been afraid to charge our rationalist/materialist/mercantile culture with depleting the quality of human life. . . . Leaders of New Age movements have stepped into the vacancy created by the church's prophetic silence: they call plastic plastic and poison poison in a society whose economy is built on convincing people that both are good for them."[5] "Today it is non-Christians who are taking seriously the demands of justice and equality, the demands of the material universe itself, and the responsibility for creating a new order. The Christian social ethic seems to be in exile."[6]

The popularity of the new religious groups is in part explained by their experience-over-knowledge orientation. They disparage thinking, denigrate the mind, ridicule education and wallow in subjective experience. Rajneesh advises: "Follow your feelings." Apostle Stevens of the Church of the Living Word emphasized that "revelation doesn't come through reasoning." His disdain for doctrine and reliance on subjective experience are illustrated by this quote from one of his sermons: "We acquire things not so much by our intellect, as by the revelation to our spirit. When we get our spirit open, then things begin to happen."[7]

Things *do* happen in aberrant Christian groups. Experientially oriented people go where the action is. They allow phenomena to determine their faith instead of interpreting experience in the light of Scripture. "We put a premium on spiritual experience," admits an ex-elder of Seattle's Community Chapel. "Once you're out in the realm of experience, you can't talk Scripture anymore because there's no Scripture that's relevant." Martyn Lloyd-Jones once remarked, "People have assumed, because the name of Christ has been used in a meeting, that all that happens in it must be truly Christian, and is, therefore, a guarantee of the soundness of all that is taught. For them the results guarantee everything."[8] The words of Jesus underscore the need to discern spiritual phenomena: "Many will say to me on that day, 'Lord, did we not prophesy in your name, and in your name drive out demons and perform many miracles?' Then I will tell them plainly, 'I never knew you. Away from me, you evildoers!' " (Mt 7:22-23).

The cultic pattern downplays the mind; the biblical pattern values understanding and knowledge. "The Bible not only respects the mind as an important part of the image of God in which man was created, but regards rational thought as a virtual gateway to salvation."[9] Satan's strategy is to subvert the mind and subdue the will into passivity, thus opening the door to spirits of deception.

Cultic religion often deprecates individuality; the person is submerged in a sea of uniformity in which individual identity is sacrificed to the goals of the group. In his classic study of the true believer, Eric Hoffer speaks of "the effacement of individual separateness."[10] An ex-member of Faith Tabernacle describes it as "total annihilation of the self" in order to become a robot for the leader. "If I could destroy my personality as such and in some mysterious way merge my life and existence with that of the group so that I as a person no longer existed, I would be free from problems."

This same unbiblical notion was preached by John Robert Stevens of the Walk, who announced that "the day of individuality is ending. Christ is coming to be glorified in His saints, not that a lot of individuals will be running around with Christ glorified in them, but that they will lose their own identity as saints. . . . God does not seem interested in giving His people anything as individuals to make them happy and contented. . . . God does not want to protract the problem of individuality."[11]

The attempt to extinguish individuality is another example of a not-so-subtle move to consolidate control. Submission, total obedience, subjection—these are the hallmarks of cultism. In the cults, submission becomes a value and an end in itself, as Peter Marin notes in his excellent essay on spiritual obedience:

There are many things to which man or woman might submit; to his own work, to the needs of others, to the love of others, to passion, to experience, to the rhythms of nature—the list is endless. . . . But that general appetite is twisted and used tyrannically when we are asked to submit ourselves unconditionally to other *persons*—whether they wear the masks of the state or of the spirit. In both instances our primary relation is no longer to the world or to others; it is to "the master," and the world or others suffer from that choice.[12]

Christians are shocked at the submission demanded by a Jim Jones or a Sun Myung Moon, but do they perceive the impending danger of a growing authoritarianism within their own ranks? Leaders require followers and are, at least in part, fashioned by their followers. Are Christians guilty of making evangelical gurus out of certain popular leaders, heeding their words, slogans and principles as much as God's Word? David Gill issues a call for discernment among Christians because demagoguery is on the loose:

There are some in our human family—and some in our Christian church—who do indeed have the charm, presence, charisma, and ability to persuade, inspire, and motivate groups of people. There is a fine line between the proper use and the abuse of such personal powers. . . . We want heroes! We want reassurance that someone knows what is going on in this mad world. We want a father or a mother to lean on. We want revolutionary folk heroes who will tell us what to do until the rapture.[13]

Christians must beware of those who demand unquestioned loyalty and seek to control the private lives of people in their charge. A good shepherd leads but does not control. He is a resource for the truth seeker, but not the ultimate source of truth. His flock must be encouraged to emulate the Bereans of the Bible who "examined the Scriptures every day to see if what Paul said was true" (Acts 17:11).

Finally, the very cult groups which claim they are targets of persecution and are in danger of losing First Amendment guarantees of religious liberty are guilty of limiting freedom of speech and stifling dissent. In his carefully documented study of Scientology, Professor Roy Wallis describes that movement's displeasure with members who question or doubt. It is the duty of the followers "to *receive* the doctrine, not to question it. Hence, the movement's literature warns against doubt, questioning, criticism, and open-mindedness."[14]

Defectors from Scientology who openly criticize the movement invite the wrath of their former mentors. The minister of public affairs of San Diego's Church of Scientology was quoted in a newspaper article as stating: "When they attack us we stop them. We stop an individual by exposing his crimes. When someone openly attacks the Church of Scientology they are committing felonies."[15] Wallis cites a Scientology document on "enemies" of the movement (who are labeled "suppressive persons") which states that "the homes, property, places and abodes of persons who have been active in attempting to suppress Scientology or Scientologists are all beyond any protection of Scientology Ethics."[16]

Sponsors of a seminar on extremist cults and youth were subjected to intimidation through letters, phone calls and personal visits. In the name of "freedom of religion" and "freedom of speech," attempts were made to prevent the convening of the seminar and, ironically, the exercise of those very freedoms. The Alliance for the Preservation of Religious Liberty (APRL), with links to well-known cults, repeatedly telephoned the administrators of the college where I teach in an attempt to discourage me from speaking to a parents' organization regarding the cults. An official of APRL allegedly tried to dissuade the manager of the conference site from contracting rooms to the sponsoring organization. On the day of the meeting, we were greeted by masked and costumed picketers carrying placards which announced that we were "anti-religious" and opposed to freedom of religion.

Activists in the so-called anticult circles have been harassed, intimidated and falsely accused by anonymous groups and individuals. Public meetings devoted to a discussion of new religious groups have been disrupted. Pastors who have scheduled seminars on the cults have been threatened. Journalists who have written about controversial groups have been sued for libel. A psychiatric social worker who has worked with former cult members received a bouquet of red roses, including a card "thanking her for her efforts to destroy religion and signed the American Nazi Party."[17]

These incidents are evidence, if indeed more is needed, that we are engaged in spiritual warfare. What we are seeing is a reminder of Paul's comments to Timothy: "Evil men and imposters will go from bad to worse, deceiving and being deceived" (2 Tim 3:13). What advice does Paul have in the face of such spiritual darkness? "Continue in what you have learned and have become convinced of" (v. 14).

As never before, Christians need to develop discernment skills. We have an obligation to be alert, informed and always ready to confront the spirit of error—wherever we may find it. We must pray daily, "Deliver us from the evil one" (Mt 6:13). At the same time, Christians must not fear God's adversary. The believer is secure and free from the power of Satan ("the evil one does not touch him"—1 Jn 5:18). "The one who is in you is greater than the one who is in the world" (1 Jn 4:4). Or, as Frederick Leahy puts it, "The unbelieving world is in Satan's embrace, but the Christian is in the arms of the Saviour."[18]

"For everyone born of God has overcome the world. This is the victory that has overcome the world, even our faith" (1 Jn 5:4).

Notes

Chapter 1
[1]James S. Gordon, "Jim Jones and His People," *New York Times Book Review,* January 7, 1979, p. 28.

Chapter 2
[1]Margaret Thaler Singer, "Coming Out of the Cults," *Psychology Today* 12, no. 8 (January 1979): 72.
[2]Roy Wallis, "The Cult and Its Transformation," in Roy Wallis, ed., *Sectarianism* (New York: John Wiley & Sons, 1975), p. 36.
[3]Rodney Stark and William Sims Bainbridge, *The Future of Religion: Secularization, Revival and Cult Formation* (Berkeley: University of California Press, 1985), p. 25.
[4]Brooks Alexander, "What Is a Cult?" *Spiritual Counterfeits Project Newsletter* 5, no. 1 (January/February 1979).
[5]Flo Conway and Jim Siegelman, *Snapping* (Philadelphia: J. B. Lippincott, 1978), p. 19.
[6]Harris Langford, *Traps: A Probe of Those Strange New Cults* (Montgomery, Ala.: Presbyterian Church in America, 1977), p. 82.
[7]Mark Albrecht, "Guru Ma Comes to Town," *Spiritual Counterfeits Project Newsletter* 5, no. 1 (January/February 1979).
[8]*Spiritual Counterfeits Project Newsletter* 2, no. 5 (June/July 1976).

[9]Stark and Bainbridge, *Future of Religion*, pp. 30, 408.

Chapter 3
[1]Alan Tobey, "The Summer Solstice of the Healthy-Happy-Holy Organization," in Charles Y. Glock and Robert N. Bellah, eds., *The New Religious Consciousness* (Berkeley: University of California Press, 1976), p. 5.
[2]*Divine Principle* (New York: The Holy Spirit Association for the Unification of World Christianity, 1973), p. 135.
[3]Ibid., p. 136.
[4]*World Government News* no. 8 (August 1978).
[5]*World Government News* no. 9 (September 1978).
[6]*The Coming Revolution in Higher Consciousness* (Pasadena: Summit Lighthouse, 1977), p. 61.
[7]John Robert Stevens, *Deception, Revelation, and Intercession*, February 2, 1975, p. 4.
[8]John Robert Stevens, *Digging the Wells* (North Hollywood, Calif.: Living Word Publications, 1969), n.p.
[9]John Robert Stevens, *School of the Prophets*, December 29, 1974, pp. 11-12.
[10]Sydney E. Ahlstrom, "From Sinai to the Golden Gate: The Liberation of Religion in the Occident," in Jacob Needleman and George Baker, eds., *Understanding the New Religions* (New York: Seabury Press, 1978), p. 6.
[11]Eldon G. Ernst, "Dimensions of New Religion in American History," in Needleman and Baker, eds., *Understanding the New Religions*, p. 44.
[12]*Spiritual Counterfeits Project Newsletter* 4, no. 6 (October/November 1978).
[13]Harvey Cox, *Turning East* (New York: Simon and Schuster, 1977), p. 100.
[14]Theodore Roszak, "Ethics, Ecstasy, and the Study of New Religions," in Needleman and Baker, eds., *Understanding the New Religions*, p. 52.
[15]Stark and Bainbridge, *Future of Religion*, p. 44.
[16]Conway and Siegelman, *Snapping*, p. 19.
[17]David Fetcho, "In the Face of the Tempest, Jonah Sleeps," *Radix* 10, no. 5 (March/April 1979): 3.

Chapter 4
[1]Ethel Grodzins Romm, "The Yinning of America," *The Humanist* 34, no. 5 (September/October 1974): 6.
[2]Martin E. Marty, *A Nation of Behavers* (Chicago: University of Chicago Press, 1976), p. 132.
[3]Ibid., p. 144.
[4]*New Age Frontiers*, June 1971.
[5]*New Age Frontiers*, January 1971.
[6]Martin E. Marty, "Religious Cause, Religious Cure," *Christian Century* 96, no. 7 (February 28, 1979): 212.
[7]J. Milton Yinger, "Countercultures and Social Change," *American Sociological*

Review 42, no. 6 (December 1977): 838.
[8]Ibid., p. 839.
[9]Eric E. Rofes, "I Was Brainwashed by the Followers of Rev. Sun Myung Moon (But I Wised Up)," *The Harvard Crimson,* September 30, 1975, p. 3.
[10]Romm, "The Yinning of America," p. 8.
[11]Patricia Thomas, "Targets of the Cults," *Human Behavior* 8, no. 3 (March 1979): 58.
[12]Stark and Bainbridge, *Future of Religion,* p. 395.

Chapter 5
[1]Eric Hoffer, *The True Believer* (New York: Harper and Bros., 1951), p. 117.
[2]Ibid., p. 119.
[3]Alan W. Scheflin and Edward M. Opton, Jr., *The Mind Manipulators* (New York: Paddington Press, 1978), p. 42.
[4]K. J. Ratnam, as quoted in Scheflin and Opton, *Mind Manipulators,* p. 43.
[5]James S. Gordon, "Jim Jones and His People," p. 28.
[6]Phil Tracy, "Jim Jones: The Making of a Madman," *New West* 3, no. 26 (December 18, 1978), p. 46.
[7]Mel White, *Deceived* (Old Tappan, New Jersey: Spire Books, 1979), p. 57.
[8]Quoted in Ronald M. Enroth, *Youth, Brainwashing and the Extremist Cults* (Grand Rapids, Mich.: Zondervan, 1977), p. 106.
[9]Ibid., p. 121.
[10]White, *Deceived,* p. 62.
[11]Peter Marin, "Spiritual Obedience," *Harper's* 258, no. 1545 (February 1979): 44.
[12]Norman R. DePuy, "Jesus and Jimmy Jones," *The American Baptist,* February 1979, p. 43.
[13]Dusty Sklar, *Gods and Beasts: The Nazis and the Occult* (New York: Thomas Y. Crowell, 1977), p. 56.
[14]Stevens, *School of the Prophets,* p. 13.
[15]John Robert Stevens, *Infallible?* January 30, 1977, pp. 12-15.
[16]"Prophecy to John Robert Stevens," *Feast of Tabernacles,* October 3, 1971, p. 7.
[17]Sklar, *Gods and Beasts,* p. 166.
[18]Ibid., p. 169.

Chapter 6
[1]Tracy, "Jim Jones: The Making of a Madman," pp. 47-48.
[2]White, *Deceived,* p. 112.

Chapter 7
[1]*Spiritual Counterfeits Project Newsletter* 5, no. 1 (January/February 1979).
[2]Marty, *A Nation of Behavers,* p. 143.
[3]*Divine Principle* (New York: The Holy Spirit Association for the Unification of World Christianity, 1973), p. 9

[4]Ibid., p. 14.
[5]Ibid., p. 132.
[6]Frederick Sontag, *Sun Myung Moon and the Unification Church* (Nashville: Abingdon, 1977), p. 101.
[7]*Divine Principle*, p. 16.
[8]Ibid., p. 10.
[9]John Robert Stevens, *The First Principles* (North Hollywood, Calif.: Living Word Publications, 1958), n.p.
[10]*Spiritual Counterfeits Project Newsletter* 2, no. 7 (September 1976).
[11]Stevens, *School of the Prophets*, pp. 3-4.
[12]Stevens, *Deception, Revelation, and Intercession*, p. 4.
[13]Stevens, *School of the Prophets*, p. 11.
[14]John Robert Stevens, *Deeper Worship* (North Hollywood, Calif.: Living Word Publications, 1975), p. 100.
[15]Stevens, *Deception, Revelation, and Intercession*, p. 2.
[16]Ibid., p. 3.
[17]Sontag, *Sun Myung Moon and the Unification Church*, p. 135.
[18]Ibid.
[19]Ibid.
[20]*New Hope News*, February 8, 1975.
[21]*New Hope News*, May 12, 1975.
[22]*New Age Frontiers*, April 1972.
[23]*New Age Frontiers*, February-March 1971.
[24]Sontag, *Sun Myung Moon and the Unfication Church*, p. 193.
[25]Ibid., pp. 144-46.
[26]*Spiritual Counterfeits Project Newsletter* 5, no. 1 (January/February 1979).

Chapter 8
[1]J. Isamu Yamamoto, *The Puppet Master* (Downers Grove, Ill.: InterVarsity Press, 1977), p. 129.
[2]*Los Angeles Times*, March 9, 1979.
[3]White, *Deceived*, p. 132.
[4]Tracy, "Jim Jones: The Making of a Madman," pp. 47-48.
[5]*Time*, August 22, 1977, p. 48.
[6]"The Children of God: Disciples of Deception," *Christianity Today*, February 18, 1977, p. 20.
[7]Ibid., p. 21.
[8]Francine J. Daner, *The American Children of Krsna* (New York: Holt, Rinehart and Winston, 1976), p. 67.
[9]Ibid., p. 68.
[10]Marin, "Spiritual Obedience," p. 51.
[11]Conway and Siegelman, *Snapping*, p. 23.
[12]Ibid., p. 33.

[13]Ibid.

[14]"Children of God: Disciples of Deception," p. 20. 15.

[15]These and the quotations immediately preceding are from various transcribed speeches of Mr. Moon collectively known as *Master Speaks,* not generally available to the public.

[16]*New Age Frontiers,* May 1972.

[17]John Robert Stevens, *What Is a Bless-In?* 1972, pp. 21, 8.

[18]Ibid., p. 13.

[19]Stevens, *Deception, Revelation, and Intercession,* p. 3.

[20]Stevens, *What Is a Bless-In?* p. 10.

[21]Ibid., p. 11.

[22]Stevens, *School of the Prophets,* p. 39.

[23]John Robert Stevens, Lesson 15, "Signs and Gifts," in *School of the Prophets,* 1975, pp. 17-29.

[24]Mark Albrecht and Brooks Alexander, "Jonestown Once More," *Spiritual Counterfeits Project Newsletter* 5, no. 1 (January/February 1979).

[25]Douglas R. Groothuis, *Unmasking the New Age* (Downers Grove, Ill.: InterVarsity Press, 1986), p. 160.

Chapter 9

[1]*The Inn Gathering* 1 no. 3, n.d.

[2]Quoted in "Children of God: Disciples of Deception," p. 21.

[3]Ronald M. Enroth, "Cult/Countercult," *Eternity,* November 1977, pp. 19, 22.

[4]Quoted in ibid., p. 22.

[5]Singer, "Coming Out of the Cults," p. 75.

[6]Stark and Bainbridge, *Future of Religion,* p. 395.

[7]Ibid., pp. 398-400.

Chapter 10

[1]Stevens, *The First Principles,* lesson 29.

[2]*Divine Principle,* p. 534.

[3]Ibid., p. 533.

[4]*New Age Frontiers,* June 1971.

[5]*New Age Frontiers,* May 1971.

[6]Ibid.

[7]*Master Speaks,* n.d.

[8]*Christianity Today,* September 7, 1984, p. 56.

[9]Joseph M. Hopkins, "Meeting the Moonies on Their Territory," *Christianity Today,* August 18, 1978, p. 41.

[10]Langford, *Traps,* pp. 185-86.

[11]John R. W. Stott, *Guard the Gospel* (Downers Grove, Ill.: InterVarsity Press, 1973), p. 91.

[12]*Spiritual Counterfeits Project Newsletter* 2, no. 7 (September 1976).

[13]Ibid.
[14]White, *Deceived*, p. 27.

Chapter 11
[1]Glock and Bellah, eds., *New Religious Consciousness*, p. 355.
[2]Irving Louis Horowitz, "Sun Myung Moon: Missionary to Western Civilization," in Irving Louis Horowitz, ed., *Science, Sin, and Scholarship* (Cambridge, Mass.: MIT Press, 1978), p. xviii.
[3]Ibid., p. xiv.
[4]Singer, "Coming out of the Cults," p. 72.
[5]Erving Goffman, *Asylums* (New York: Doubleday, 1961), p. 15.
[6]Horowitz, *Science, Sin, and Scholarship*, p. xiii.
[7]Ibid., p. xiv.
[8]*New Age Frontiers*, January 1971.
[9]"Investigation of Korean-American Relations," Report of the Subcommittee on International Organizations of the Committee on International Relations, U.S. House of Representatives, October 31, 1978, pp. 387-88.
[10]Horowitz, *Science, Sin, and Scholarship*, p. xvii.
[11]David Haddon and Vail Hamilton, *TM Wants You!* (Grand Rapids, Mich.: Baker, 1976), p. 21.
[12]*TM in Court* (Berkeley, Calif.: Spiritual Counterfeits Project, 1978), p. vii.
[13]*Los Angeles Times*, August 19, 1978.
[14]*Billings Gazette*, September 27, 1978.
[15]Chris Welks, "The Eclipse of Sun Myung Moon," in Horowitz, ed., *Science, Sin, and Scholarship*, p. 252.
[16]Ibid., p. 251.
[17]*Sacramento Union*, March 11, 1979.
[18]*Fort Wayne Journal-Gazette*, March 11, 1979.

Chapter 12
[1]*New Religious Movements Newsletter* 1, no. 2 (March 1979).
[2]*Los Angeles Times*, March 9, 1979.
[3]Ibid.
[4]Barbara W. Hargrove, "Some Thoughts About the Unification Movement and the Churches," in Horowitz, ed., *Science, Sin, and Scholarship*, p. 98.
[5]Fetcho, "In the Face of the Tempest, p. 3.
[6]Kenneth Leech, *Youthquake* (Totowa, N.J.: Littlefield, Adams, 1977), p. 207.
[7]Stevens, *What is a Bless-In?* p. 16.
[8]Quoted in Frederick S. Leahy, *Satan Cast Out* (Edinburgh: Banner of Truth Trust, 1975), p. 166.
[9]*The God-Men* (Berkeley, Calif.: Spiritual Counterfeits Project, 1977), p. 68.
[10]Hoffer, *The True Believer*, p. 66.
[11]John Robert Stevens, *From Many Comes One*, May 29, 1977, pp. 3, 15.

[12]Marin, "Spiritual Obedience," p. 4.

[13]David W. Gill, "Leaders and Demagogues," *Radix* 10, no. 4 (January/February 1979).

[14]Roy Wallis, *The Road to Total Freedom: A Sociological Analysis of Scientology* (New York: Columbia University Press, 1977), p. 230.

[15]*San Diego Union,* August 14, 1977.

[16]Wallis, *Road to Total Freedom,* p. 154.

[17]Alan MacRobert, "Uncovering the Cult Conspiracy," *Mother Jones* 4, no. 11 (February/March 1979), p. 8.

[18]Leahy, *Satan Cast Out,* p. 175.

Index